Thomas Jefferson's Enlightenment

Background Notes

Thomas Jefferson's Enlightenment

Background Notes

By

James C. Thompson

Commonwealth Books

Boothbay Harbor, Maine

www.commonwealthbooks.org

Email: info@commonwealthbooks.org

Library of Congress Control Number: 2014947669

ISBN (Print): 978-0-9904018-1-0

ISBN (E-book/MobiPocket) 978-0-9904018-2-7

ISBN (E-book/EPUB) 978-0-9904018-3-4

ISBN (E-book/PDF) 978-0-9904018-4-1

Cover: Bust of Thomas Jefferson
by Jean-Antoine Houdon (1789)
Courtesy, Library of Congress Image

Printed in the United States of America

Other Books by James C. Thompson

The Birth of Virginia's Aristocracy

(2009)

Commonwealth Books of Virginia

(ISBN) 9780982592205

The Dubious Achievement of the 1st Continental Congress

(2011)

Commonwealth Books of Virginia

(ISBN) 9780982592229

Thomas Jefferson's Enlightenment – Paris 1785

(2014)

Commonwealth Books of Virginia

(ISBN) 9780985486310

To

Margaret Porch Thompson Lounsbury

Patron of the Arts

Contents

Opening Comment

*M*y earlier book, *Thomas Jefferson's Enlightenment – Paris 1785* was set in the final years of France's Ancien Régime. In it, I explained that Jefferson went to France to start his life over. I explained that he planned to reconstruct himself in the image of the marquis de Chastellux, and that as he groomed himself to join the refined company of men like Chastellux, millions of destitute French peasants starved and the decrepit French monarchy drifted into bankruptcy. They were, as Charles Dickens famously said, the best of times and the worst of times.

Jefferson met the marquis during a visit the exemplary Frenchman paid to Monticello in the spring of 1782. The visit took place in the tension-filled month prior to the birth of his sixth child. On 6 September 1782, four months after the child's birth, his wife Martha died and his world collapsed. Twenty-two months later, Jefferson departed for France. In a letter he sent to a friend in Williamsburg, Virginia on September 30, 1785, he confirmed that his private purpose for going was "to examine more nearly the condition of the great [and] to appreciate the true value of the circumstances in their situation." The world these remarkable people lived in collapsed shortly after Jefferson returned home. Some of his closest friends were murdered during the upheaval that ensued.

The story I tell in *Thomas Jefferson's Enlightenment* is about how the self-described "savage from the mountains of America" became immersed in the world's most cultivated and elegant society. This was not something he accomplished by himself. Even a brilliant man like Jefferson needed assistance in learning the manners, the values, and the ideas of the best people of France. I put him in the hands of an equally brilliant guide. In my reconstruction, Jefferson developed into a man of the world in the company of someone he actually knew. Pierre Cabanis was the one man in Paris who was familiar with all the details of the French Enlightenment, acquainted with all of the city's lumieres, and close enough to Jefferson to serve as his instructor.

I believe the political campaigns Jefferson undertook later in the 1790s were conducted by a man who was significantly different from the circumspect political loner who drafted the *Declaration of Independence* without consultation in his Philadelphia rooms. I trace his transformation from political solipsist into progressive political activist in a series of excursions in which the man who is aspiring to restart his life learns from the man who knows everything about the society he wishes to join.

Pierre Cabanis lived in the household of Madame Helvétius. Madame was also a close personal friend of Benjamin Franklin. I believe Jefferson met Cabanis through Franklin at some point before he received the printed copies of his book, *Notes on the State of Virginia*. These books arrived on 10 May 1785. In my non-fiction narrative, Jefferson's adventures with Cabanis begin shortly after that.

In their third excursion, I have Cabanis introduce Jefferson to the leader of an elite circle of reformers. Jefferson's first audience with Louis Alexandre, duc de la Rochefoucauld appears to have taken place in the fall of 1785. Prominent members of his circle were the marquis de Lafayette and the marquis de Condorcet. I believe that Jefferson's conversations with these "chateau reformers" rekindled the sentiments that underpinned his revolutionary-era mission to dismantle Virginia's colonial hierarchy.

In my narrative, the duc and the members of his circle hold the author of the *Declaration of Independence* in high esteem because they believe he knows how to frame a constitutional government with a properly structured bill of rights. As they deliberate on what rights are inherent and how to protect them in a new representative government, they consult the American expert. As they are doing this, the monarchy bumbles toward its fateful end.

Jefferson allows himself to be diverted in the fall of 1786 when American artist John Trumbull joins his household. Trumbull introduces the recently enlightened American Ambassador to English artist Richard Cosway and his charming wife. Perhaps it is because Maria Cosway is married that Jefferson ends their budding romance after only a few enchanted outings.

In the winter of 1787, Jefferson leaves Paris on a three month mind-clearing tour through the south of France and northern Italy. When he returns to the French capital in mid-June, the Assembly of Notables has completed its historic meeting and the effort is under-way to replace France's bankrupt monarchy with a constitutional government. I believe it is during this eleventh hour effort to liberate the French people from monarchical tyranny that Jefferson comes into his own. In these frantic moments, the circumspect political loner blossoms into the enlightened progressive activist. I believe the experience Jefferson gained in this effort to deliver the French people from tyranny continued to guide him after he returned home.

The first seventeen commentaries in this book contain details and supplemental information that I was unable to weave into my earlier narrative. In my closing discussion, I trace the evolution of Jeffersonian historiography through its two hundred year existence. I have included it because I want readers understand me when I say that the man they read about today is a manufactured product. During the last seventy years, the person who lived once in the real world has been largely replaced by an invention that now forms the center of a massive social engineering program.

A decade or so before the beginning of the 21st century, Jeffersonian historiographers devoted themselves to what I call legacy management. It is understandable that the managers of the new Jeffersonian legacy would avoid a man who, it seems, kept his own children as slaves. I think there is more to it, however. The business of today's Jeffersonians is to create a better world, not to remember the man. This new world is based on a Jeffersonian Philosophy of Human Rights that his legacy managers have substantially manufactured. Whether it was Jefferson's is a good deal less certain.

I present my comments on the changing Jeffersonian template because I want to distinguish the real world, day-to-day person I find interesting, from the distillations that concern contemporary Jeffersonians. Also, I want to distinguish my day-to-day approach for understanding an historical figure from big picture analyses that are used to explain Jefferson's manufactured legacy.

As a Philosopher, I think the way to learn about Jefferson is to investigate how he acquired his bright ideas: where did he encounter them, who conveyed them to him, how did he interpret them, and why did he think they were important? Analyzing Jefferson's "legacy" is not part of this enterprise. Nor is it useful for understanding the man in his time. If we want to understand Thomas Jefferson, I believe we need to learn who he knew, how he met them, what he with them, and whether he did things differently after his interactions with them.

Jefferson is worth knowing, in my opinion, because he interacted with creative people. Men he associated with helped to invent the modern world. He made a number of significant contributions to the enterprises himself. When we investigate how he interacted with these extraordinary individuals in his day-to-day affairs, we meet the real Thomas Jefferson. This is the person I follow through Paris in *Thomas Jefferson's Enlightenment,* and it is the person I discuss in the pages of this book.

James C. Thompson
Boothbay Harbor, Maine
August 2014

chapter one

Thomas Jefferson: Political Loner

*I*t may sound strange to Jeffersonians who think of Thomas Jefferson as the author of what is arguably the most important political document ever written, but during his first political career (which extended from September 1769, when Jefferson entered the Virginia House of Burgesses, to June of 1781 when his second term as Governor of the State of Virginia ended) Jefferson harbored a variety of opinions and preferences that separated him from his peers in the hierarchy of Virginia and in the patriotic party that orchestrated America's formal political separation from England in 1776.

Three Jeffersonian heterodoxies are particularly significant in the story of Thomas Jefferson's Enlightenment:

1) Jefferson was a man of Reason not a man of Faith. His reason led him to object to the orthodoxies of Virginia's Anglican Church and to its exercise of political power in the colony. Jefferson was, in other words, a "Dissenter". His peers in Virginia were not.

2) In the debate that culminated in the separation of the American colonies from England, Jefferson did not share his fellow Patriots' enthusiasm for Natural Law either as a foundation for Public Right as justification for political independence.

Yes, the author of the *Declaration of Independence* invoked the Natural Rights of Man as justification for severing political bands with England, but Jefferson was a Lawyer, not a Philosopher. He was trained to defend his clients by building cases on legal precedents. He was not trained to defend or advance theories by elucidating valid entailments and establishing logically necessary relationships between premises and conclusions.

The concept of Natural Law was in Jefferson's eyes vague and malleable compared to Common Law. As an authority in the Common Law, Jefferson found Natural Law unnecessary to accomplish the political objectives of the independence movement. He made this clear in his first political tract, which he drafted alone at Monticello in the summer of 1774.

3) Jefferson spent much of the American Revolution alone on his mountaintop devising ways to dismantle the hierarchical system that channeled the wealth and political power of Virginia into the hands of a privileged few.

In his private crusade to disempower Virginia's colonial ruling class and to make way for Virginia's new republican government and society, Jefferson was working directly against the social and financial interests of own class.

Jefferson was aware that these positions might undermine his social relationships and political opportunities. He was therefore careful to keep them to himself. Jefferson was like the Wizard of Oz, out of sight on his mountaintop, pulling levers to change the world. No one was to know what he really thought, what he was doing, or why he was doing it. Operating as he did with a Wizard-of-Oz mentality, he drafted all the notable public papers he wrote during the revolutionary period—by himself with virtually no input from others.

Let us consider his four most celebrated Revolutionary-era texts:

1) Jefferson wrote what is known today as "The Summary View of the Rights of British America" in seclusion at Monticello in July 1774. In it, Jefferson argued from precedent that Americans were a sovereign people and that the English King and English Parliament had no right to meddle in their affairs. His peers in the House of Burgesses considered his argument and rejected his claim.

2) Jefferson drafted his *Constitution for the State of Virginia* in his Philadelphia rooms in May and June of 1776. He incorporated into it a "Bill of Rights", which included the right of settlers to free and full ownership of the land they settled. He also incorporated into it a plan for proportional representation.

Giving settlers direct ownership of the land they settled was a creative way to undermine the feudal land laws that sustained Virginia's Tidewater land barons during colonial times. Proportional representation would, over time, transfer political power away from the Tidewater's aristocrats to the yeoman farmers who were filling Virginia's vacant western lands.

Jefferson was privately outraged that the members of the

Virginia Convention, which met in Williamsburg while he sat in the Second Continental Congress in Philadelphia, approved George Mason's constitution instead of his late-arriving alternative. He later vented the anger this aroused in him in Chapter 13 of his *Notes on the State of Virginia*.

3) Jefferson drafted the *Declaration of Independence* alone in his Philadelphia rooms in June 1776.

He began his draft by restating the first three propositions in George Mason's *Virginia Declaration of Rights* in which Mason referred to "the Natural Rights of enjoyment of Life and Liberty, and the means for acquiring property and pursuing Happiness."

Jefferson followed these with the 28 precedents he had used to support the argument he presented in his *Summary View of the Rights of British America*. He reused them in the preamble of his plan for the new government of Virginia. Now he used them a third time to support declaring independence from England.

The Congress revised Jefferson's preamble, crossed out a couple of Jefferson's precedents, and added a couple other notable lines before approving the document.

4) As a member of the Committee of Revisors, on which he served from January 1777 until June 1779, Jefferson drafted sixty-six Bills alone on his Charlottesville mountaintop.

Among these measures was a bill cleverly designed to change the political order in the new State of Virginia. Jefferson devised his plan for a system of public education to raise up a governing class he referred to as a "Natural Aristoi".

The members of Virginia's third General Assembly refused to enact a single one of the measures Jefferson drafted or any of the sixty-six bills his fellow committeemen drafted.

Amazingly, for only one of these four documents did Jefferson seek input—he may have consulted with George Wythe on one or two fine points for his Constitution for the State of Virginia.

This circumspect political loner was the man who sailed to France in July of 1784. I explain in *Thomas Jefferson's Enlightenment* how this political solipsist transformed during his five years in France into a progressive political leader. This new man, after he returned home, waged and won the 2nd American Revolution in the Presidential election of 1800.

chapter two

Why Did Thomas Jefferson Go to France?

*T*here are two kinds of answers to this question. What I call "the historical report answer" provides information that is factually correct, but incomplete in respect to providing a full understanding of the matter. What I call "the beyond-the-veil answer" considers the factual record in terms of the circumstances of the people involved. Because it encompasses the action, the actor(s), their circumstances, and their intentions, it presents the most complete account of the event. Not surprisingly, the historical report answers the question of why Jefferson went to Frances differently from how the beyond-the-veil answer does.

Those who examine the historical record will find that on four occasions the "Congress of the States Assembled" invited Jefferson to be one of its agents in France:

1) The Congress sent its first invitation in September of 1776 immediately after Jefferson resigned his seat in the Second Continental Congress and returned to Virginia. Writing many years later in his *Autobiography,* Jefferson explained:

   Such was the state of my family that I could not leave it, nor could I expose it to the dangers of the sea, and capture by British ships.

2) The Congress sent a second invitation immediately after Jefferson finished his second term as Governor of the State of Virginia in June 1781. In his *Autobiography,* Jefferson observed:

> *The same reasons obliged me still to decline.*

3) Congress sent a third invitation in November 1782, two months after the death of Jefferson's wife. Jefferson quickly accepted this invitation. After making his arrangements, he set out in the company of his eldest daughter to confer with the Congress in Philadelphia. He proceeded from there to Baltimore. While waiting to get under way, he received word that England had signed a treaty of peace in Paris. The reason for his mission being resolved, Jefferson returned home.

4) In March 1784, Congress sent a fourth request. Would Jefferson join John Adams and Benjamin Franklin in negotiating treaties of commerce? Again Jefferson accepted. On 5 July, he boarded a ship in Boston and departed for France in the company of his daughter Martha.

The historical report answer is therefore: Jefferson went to France as a representative of the Congress of the States United to negotiate commercial agreements with its European Trading Partners.

This is not the conclusion we reach when we peer beyond the veil. We are then able to connect the dots in the written record with the circumstances in which these events occurred. This shows us a picture of a man acting in the moment.

The first thing we notice is the event that changed Jefferson's life: the death of his wife. In her final hours, in her weak hand, Martha penned these words from *Tristram Shandy:* "the days and hours . . . are flying . . . like clouds of windy day never to return . . ."

Jefferson completed the line:

. . . every time I kiss thy hand to bid adieu, every absence which follows it, are preludes to that eternal separation which we are shortly to make.

Not long after her death, Jefferson sent a letter to the marquis de Chastellux. In it, he observed:

A single event wiped away all my plans and left me a blank, which I had not the spirits to fill up.

Jefferson inscribed on his wife's grave this wistful line from *The Iliad:*

Nay if even in the house of Hades the dead forget their dead, yet will I even there be mindful of my dear comrade.

Why would Jefferson notify Chastellux of his wife's passing? A few weeks before Martha Jefferson delivered her 6th child [Lucy Elizabeth was born on 8 May 1782], the marquis paid Jefferson a weeklong visit at Monticello. Chastellux was a member of the prestigious French Academy and had been third in command of the French forces at Yorktown. Jefferson was mesmerized by his guest's erudition and brilliant conversation, which were welcome distractions in the tension-filled weeks preceding Martha's delivery.

These considerations in mind, the beyond-the-veil answer is: Congress's third and fourth requests reached Jefferson after his world collapsed. He was in a state of despair and facing the depressing task of starting his life over alone. He thought back on the Renaissance man who had filled his gloomy home with light. Contemplating his lonely future, Jefferson decided to rebuild his life in the society that produced the marquis de Chastellux. Jefferson went to France, I believe, to become a citizen of the world like the worldly French academician. He went to France, in other words, in pursuit of personal happiness.

chapter three

Jefferson's Plan

*C*onversations about Jefferson today tend to divide between Jefferson the-father-of-Human-Rights and Jefferson the-father-of-his-slave's-children. These conversations should not prevent us from noticing how Jefferson conducted his daily affairs and accomplished his larger purposes.

Jefferson may have been a skilled patriotic draftsman and lonely after the death of his wife, but he was not an abstract thinker like, for example, John Locke or Jean-Jacques Rousseau. He exhibited instead the traits of a scientist, observing Nature and measuring, enumerating, and organizing things that he observed. Jefferson sought to create right order, precise order, where he thought things were not in proper order. Four examples of this are:

1) In the summer of 1774, alone on his mountaintop, Jefferson crystalized his objection to British rule in America. He asserted that British Americans were a sovereign people, that the hierarchical government of King George III violated the natural order, that the English king had no right to meddle in the affairs of America, and that, by right, Americans should govern themselves.

He carried this idea to the next logical step during the winter and spring of 1776 by incorporating a collection of regulations and procedures into his plan for the government for the State of Virginia.

He completed the cycle a week later by drafting a rationale for separating from England and creating independent governments in the American colonies. His argument began with the appeal to the Author of Nature that George Mason invoked in his *Virginia Declaration of Rights*. Jefferson supplemented Mason's Natural Law claims with the same list of the King and Parliament's transgressions against English and colonial law he had used in the two previously mentioned documents.

2) After declaring independence, Jefferson joined the first Virginia Assembly. As a member of this assembly, he conducted a carefully planned legislative campaign to fix what he perceived as flaws in his state's new constitution. In eight weeks, Jefferson drafted, aided in drafting, and revised more than fifteen bills. These measures included:

- A plan to change the land laws of this State,
- A plan to disestablish the Church of England,
- A plan to promote westward migration,
- Plans for implementing the State's new court system, and
- A plan for revising Virginia's outdated Colonial Code.

3) Toward the end of the first session of the First General Assembly, he was appointed to the Committee of Revisors. Jefferson spent the next two and a half years writing dozens of pieces of legislation, which he deemed necessary for the new State of Virginia to become "a well-ordered republic."

4) When Jefferson returned from France in the fall of 1789, he redesigned and reconstructed his mountaintop home and gardens to meet the needs of the Renaissance man he became in France. This enterprise occupied him for 25 years.

In this last undertaking Jefferson's true genius blossomed— as an architect and engineer. He created and implemented complex plans for some of our country's most beautiful buildings.

With the same care and precision, in the summer of 1781 Jefferson commenced work on what became his only book. His *Notes on the State of Virginia* was a detailed, comprehensive collection of facts pertaining to the natural, social, and political characteristics of his state.

Jefferson built his book around a set of responses he developed for a questionnaire circulated by the French consul in Philadelphia, marquis de Barbé-Marbois. Abandoning his revolutionary-era practice, Jefferson reached out to several individuals whom he considered knowledgeable on these matters. First among these was his compatriot in the Independence Party and fellow member of the American Philosophical Society, Charles Thomson.

On his way to board his France-bound ship in the spring of 1784, Jefferson stopped in Philadelphia. He was unable to locate his friend, but during a shopping excursion he was able to purchase "an uncommonly large panther skin." "By this means," Dumas Malone observed, "he hoped to convince Buffon that this animal and the cougar were not identical."

What was Malone referring to? Jefferson publicly praised the arrogant French naturalist as "the best informed of any naturalist who has ever written." Privately, Jefferson was outraged by an amazing error he found in Buffon's work. According to Buffon, Jefferson observed, the animals common both to the old and new world were smaller in the latter. Buffon gave two reasons for this: 1) the heat in America was less; and 2) water covered more land in North America than in Europe.

Offended by the French scientist's slight to his homeland, Jefferson dedicated himself to refuting Buffon's erroneous theory. While assembling the facts of the matter, it dawned on him that he could use his work to support his private mission. By gifting copies of his finished critique to individuals in Chastellux's lettered circle, Jefferson might establish himself as a peer in their eyes.

When the savage from the mountains of America reached Paris, his first call was on his former congressional colleague, Benjamin Franklin, who was then American Ambassador to the Court of King Louis XVI. During this visit, Jefferson acquired from Franklin the name of his printer. Nine months later, having transformed the loose pages of information he had been accumulating for two and half years into a manuscript, Jefferson had Franklin's printer print 200 copies.

He gifted about thirty of these to French cognoscenti and to acquaintances elsewhere in Europe. He sent 145 copies to friends in America—more than half in boxes to Madison and Wythe. Some of these appear to have been sold. Others were apparently distributed to selected students at Jefferson's alma mater in Williamsburg, Virginia.

Jefferson replaced Franklin as American Ambassador in July of 1785. As America's new ambassador, Jefferson was welcomed into the best circles of Parisian society. In this mundane way, the savage from the American mountains achieved his private objective. His book passed out of his mind as his social connections solidified. In a letter to the marquis de Chastellux on 7 June 1785, he confirmed that he was having second thoughts about his book. Would his comments on slavery and Virginia's constitution "do more harm than good?" he wondered. He later acknowledged that the project that had occupied so much of his time during his first nine months in France, produced more headaches than benefits.

chapter four

A Brief History of 18th Century France

rance's monarchy was in dire straits when Jefferson landed at La Harve in the summer of 1784. It had been bankrupted by a century of periodic wars and the uninterrupted profligacy of its kings. To under-stand the circumstances of France when Jefferson arrived, it is sufficient to trace events from the year 1756. In that year, war broke out between France and England over the boundaries that separated their North American territories.

Known as "The French and Indian War" in America, the conflict quickly spread to Europe where it was known as "The Seven Years War". In this theater of the conflict, Austria aligned with France against Prussia. English imperialist William Pitt, then Secretary of the Northern Department, perceiving this as an opportunity to advance Britain's colonial interests, solicited Parliament to supply Prussia with 16,000 troops from George II's Hanoverian homeland. These troops arrived in Prussia in 1757. When France turned east to battle the wily king of Prussia, Pitt unleashed England's powerful navy to attack France's colonies in the four corners of the world—Canada, the East Indies and the Philippines, India, and Africa. Miraculously, the English assaults on all of these French colonies were successful.

The conflict was raging when England's old king died in 1760. German-born George II was succeeded by his English-born grandson. Seeing no advantage in pursing Pitt's diversion on the European Continent, George III immediately set about making peace. Negotiations between France and England culminated in the Treaty of Paris, which brought an end to the French and Indian War in February 1763. The Treaty of Hubertusburg, signed by Prussia and Austria, ended the Seven Years War in the same month.

England emerged from this global conflict the most powerful nation in the world. The Mistress of the Seas controlled Canada in North America, The Philippines, and other French possessions in Africa, India, and the East Indies. While this ignited an economic boom in England, France languished under massive war debts, which it had no prospects for settling.

Profligate King Louis XV died at Versailles in May 1774. He was succeeded by his grandson. Louis XVI was not yet twenty when he ascended to the French throne.

Minister of Marine, comte de Maurepas, advised the new king in forming his first government. The jaded old courtier had developed an extensive network of connections during his twenty-four years in service to Louis XV. His first recommendation was to place the comte de Vergennes at the head of the Ministry of State. In this post, Vergennes would direct France's foreign affairs. Maurepas then recommended that abbé de Terray be retained as Comptroller General and that Monsieur Turgot be made the Minister of Marine.

Two other recommendations that are consequential to the story of Jefferson's enlightenment were that Georges Louis Leclerc, comte de Buffon, be confirmed as Intendant of the King's Garden and that Buffon be given authority to expand that institution into a center of scientific research.

When the new government was first established, Vergennes answered to Maurepas. This changed, however, as Vergennes gained influence with the young king. The realignment became permanent soon after adventurous Pierre-Augustin Caron de Beaumarchais sent his famous missive to the king. In it, the anonymous author implored the young monarch to aid the floundering American rebellion against England. Delivered in the summer of 1775, the letter read in part:

You will only preserve the peace you desire, Sire, by preventing an accord from being made between England and America, and by preventing one of these from completely triumphing over the other. The only means for attaining this end is to give assistance to the Americans that allows them to put their forces on an equal footing with those of England. Believe me, Sire, the economy of a few millions now will, before long, cost a great deal more in the blood and money of France. [Louis de Loménie. *Beaumarchais and his times: Sketches of French society in the eighteenth century.* Translated by Henry S. Edwards. Addey & Company. London. 1856. 122.]

During the fall of 1775, a direct correspondence opened between Vergennes and Monsieur Beaumarchais. The question now became: how should France assist the American rebellion? The minister suggested that one million livres might find their way into a trading company that might buy surplus French arms, but he made it clear that Beaumarchais would have to direct the business and bear all the risk. In the spring of 1776, Beaumarchais formed Roderigue Hortalez et Cie and began to funnel arms and military supplies to the American insurgents using funds provided by the nearly bankrupt French government.

L'abbé Terray had kept his post in the old government by supplying King Louis XV with whatever money the king wished to spend. Terray covered the yearly deficits with loans that grew in size each year. This was the way things had been done for many decades, and Maurepas was satisfied to let it continue. He might have allowed Terray to mismanage the country's finances forever had his wife not forced Turgot upon him. After resisting for a month, Maurepas gave in and recommended that Turgot be moved from Minister of Marine to Comptroller General of Finance.

During his brief tenure as Minister of Marine, Turgot acquainted himself with the King's grave financial circumstances. In a memorandum he wrote before accepting the new post, Turgot warned the king that "the first gunshot" would force the state into bankruptcy. Turgot agreed to accept the post, however, and lead the nation away from its financial cliff if the King would grant him the power to implement a far-reaching plan. Then, Turgot vowed, he would solve France's financial problems without increasing taxes or borrowing more money. Said Turgot: "No bankruptcy, No new taxes, No new loans!"

Young King Louis XVI promised his steadfast support. "Fear nothing," the young king assured Turgot. "I will always sustain you!" Turgot began his service as France's chief financial officer in August 1774.

During thirteen years as Intendant of France's impoverished Limoge district, Turgot had applied economic concepts that he borrowed from Jacques Claude Marie Vincent de Gournay and Francois Quesnay.

As Louis XV's physician, Quesnay had the king's ear. In addition to giving him advice on matters relating to his personal health, Quesnay counseled the impetuous monarch on his mounting financial difficulties. Wealth would be created and the kingdom returned to economic health, Quesnay advised, by lifting regulations that restricted free trade in corn. He distilled his recommendation into this famous maxim: "poor peasant, poor kingdom; poor kingdom, poor king!"

As Comptroller General, a significant part of Turgot's program to restore France to economic health involved implementing Quesnay's ideas, which were being refined by a group of economists who called themselves *Phsyiocrats*. Prominent among these men was Pierre Samuel du Pont de Nemours. As a younger man, du Pont had been

Quesnay's protégé. When Turgot became Comptroller General, he appointed du Pont as his deputy. Du Pont would perform "quantitative analyses" on the policies Turgot proposed so the Comptroller General could understand their financial impact on the economy and government revenue.

Turgot intended to restore France to economic health by reducing expenditures below revenues enough to realize an annual saving of twenty million *livres.* To accomplish this, he directed His Majesty to order the heads of all departments of the royal government to "concert" with the Minister of Finance. As his ministerial colleagues brought their budgets into fiscal order, Turgot planned to introduce a series of reforms, which he would implement by the authority of the King. First, he would simplify the operation of the government by eliminating redundant and conflicting regulations. Then he would remove corrupt officials, abolish monopolistic practices and institutions, and replace the existing method of taxation and tax collection.

Once these measures to streamline and purify the government were under way, Turgot intended to implement a set of positive policies to promote the flow of public and private capital into economically productive areas. Doing these things would unfetter the nation's entrepreneurial *bourgeoisie,* which would rush forward in pursuit of its own prosperity. Physiocrats called this approach *laissez-faire:* when industrious people are permitted to pursue their own interests, they produce things, whether in agriculture, industry, or commerce, that enhance the well-being of the community.

Not surprisingly, Turgot's plan met with opposition from those with "vested interests". Unfortunately, this group included *everyone* in the hierarchy of the kingdom. By the summer of 1776, the clamor had become so great that the King could no longer endure it. Buckling under relentless pressure from the queen, he requested Turgot's resignation.

Turgot's fall accelerated Vergennes' rise. The shift had been fore-shadowed in the spring of the previous year when Vergennes wrote the King about France's naval relations with Spain. "I am aware, sire of the state of your navy, but I have no idea of the situation of your finances." By the summer of 1776, in other words, it was no longer possible to conduct France's foreign policy without also engaging in its domestic finances.

Maurepas' last consequential act was to nominate Swiss banker Jacques Necker to fill Turgot's empty chair. The king consented to this, and Necker was called to direct the nation's finances. Necker went on to scrap most of Turgot's program and return to the policy of borrowing that abbé Terray had followed. Necker took up his duties as clouds gathered over North America.

Over the next four years, France appears to have contributed nearly 300 million livres to the American war effort. J. B. Perkins offered this assessment in *France in the American Revolution:*

France had just gotten through the third campaign of the alliance at an outlay of one hundred and fifty million livres, and the fourth campaign bade fair to cost much more. At this era of

discouragement, the Spanish were strenuous in their advice that
France should get such terms as she could for her American allies
and make peace without more delay. [Perkins. New York.
Houghton Mifflin. 1911. 326–327.]

Whether it was 150 million livres or twice that amount, Vergennes understood that the financial burden was beyond France's ability to support. He was therefore determined to secure its repayment. He imagined this could be done with a combination of loan liquidation and new revenue derived from trade.

Vergennes enlisted du Pont to analyze the economies of the thirteen states and to prepare an estimate of the revenues France might generate through trade with the new American states. Du Pont had not yet set foot in America, but he had applied Quesnay's analytical methods for the intendant of Soissons and for Turgot. Now he applied them in his most consequential project.

Du Pont began by preparing an outline for his analysis in which he listed the components involved. He called on the reigning expert on matters pertaining to geography, climate, and zoology—comte de Buffon. Du Pont's analyses, in keeping with his training under Quesnay, were heavily weighted toward agriculture and the movement of grains and other agricultural products. Structures of government, government regulations, modes of transportation, population size, and population distribution were germane to these analyses. To acquire this information about America, du Pont, perhaps with assistance from Buffon's staff, developed a questionnaire.

Vergennes then directed that this questionnaire be sent to the governors of the American states. Jefferson was among the men who responded to this questionnaire.

Bear in mind that when Jefferson arrived in France the monarchy was bankrupt. Its ability to function depended on the repayment of the loans it made to America during its revolution and on an expansion of trade with its American ally. By 1784, hope for repayment of the loans had dwindled and the revenues from trade remained miniscule. Reformers viewed the revolution in America as a step in the march of human progress and contemplated ways to duplicate it in France. By the winter of 1786, Thomas Jefferson was counseling the duc de la Rochefoucauld and the members of his small circle on how a new constitutional government would embody the unalienable rights of the people. As he did, petit bourgeoisie malcontents in the political clubs of the Palais Royal began developing their own plans.

chapter five

Jefferson's Paris

*T*wo thousand years before Jefferson arrived in France, natives established the first settlement in the area of what is now the French capital. It was an encampment on the island that 2,000 years later is the center of the largest metropolis in Europe. Through most of its history, the community was walled. With each phase of its expansion, from encampment to hamlet, from hamlet to village, from village to town, from town to city, its defensive wall was rebuilt and enlarged. In the 1630s, Louis XIII enlarged the wall again, extending the barrier Charles V had built in the 1370s. Louis XIII's addition encompassed growth that took place in the first half of the 17th century. Growth continued after Louis XIII's addition. By the beginning of the 18th century, the population of Paris had risen toward 450,000 and was again beyond the city's wall.

Fearing that continued growth would undermine the balance he perceived between the city's physical beauty and its social order, Louis XIII's son developed a plan to prevent it from expanding further. As Louis XIV moved to limit his capital's growth, he commenced an ambitious urban beautification program. This program began early in the 1700s with the removal of Louis XIII's barrier. The wall-builder's son did this in the belief that his military successes had made the city safe from invasion. When Jefferson reached Paris, a beautiful boulevard, known as le Cours ou le Boulevard, filled the space that Louis XIII's wall had formerly occupied. Louis XIV's no-growth decree notwithstanding, the population of the city had risen to 550,000, and its thoroughfares were clogged with vehicles, goods, and people.

Two years before Jefferson's arrival, Louis XVI authorized the directors of his tax agency to erect yet another barrier. Unlike its predecessors, the Wall of the Farmers-General was not intended as a system of defense. Its purpose was to facilitate the collection of public revenue. Construction of this *cloture* began shortly after Jefferson took up residence at the Hôtel Landron in October of 1784. What Jefferson referred to as a "wall of circumvallation" was to consist of sixteen elegant toll-collection stations situated between the city's forty-seven "gates". Had it been completed, this barrier would have doubled the size of the city to approximately 3440 hectares, thirteen square English miles.

Viewed on a map, the Wall of the Farmers-General looks something like an egg. This egg was bisected on its North-South axis by two conjoining avenues—rue Saint Martin meets rue Saint Jacques at the Seine. It was bisected on its East-West axis by a sequence of three avenues: rue de Roule on the west, rue Saint-Honoré in the center, and rue Saint Antoine on the right. The oldest part of Paris lies near the intersection of the two axes.

When Jefferson arrived, Ile de la Cite was home to the city's court system and its Bureau of Police. Le Palais de Justice occupied the western end of the island. "The mother of the church of France" occupied its eastern end. Adjacent to the Cathedral of Notre Dame was the Hôtel Dieu, the city's oldest hospital.

In 1702, Louis XIV divided his capital into twenty *quartiers*. This plan was not amended until the eve of the Revolution when it was updated to facilitate the nomination and election of deputies to the Estates-General. The city was then repartitioned into sixty districts. (The year after Jefferson's departure, the city was redistricted into forty-eight sections. In 1795, these sections were consolidated into the first twelve of the city's current arrondissements.)

Le Quartier Ile de la Cite was the first of Louis XIV's twenty quartiers. During Jefferson's time, it was ringed by eleven *faubourgs*. The word "faubourg" is derived from the Latin words *foris burgem*, which means "outside the city". Eight of these faubourgs lay on the north side of the Seine. The remaining three were on its south side. The city's northwestern quadrant included Faubourg de Saint Honoré, Faubourg de Le Roule, Faubourg de Montmartre, Faubourg de Poinsoniere, and Faubourg de Saint Denis. Its northeastern quadrant included Faubourg de Saint Martin, Faubourg de Temple, and Faubourg de Saint Antoine. Its southeastern quadrant contained Faubourg de Saint Jacques and Faubourg de Saint Marcel. Its southwestern quadrant consisted of Faubourg de Saint Germain.

Like most other high-ranking government officials and foreign dignitaries, Jefferson chose to live in the city's northwestern sector. During the two decades preceding Jefferson's arrival, much of the open ground in the northern tier of this sector was developed—both of Jefferson's Parisian residences were built during this period. Hôtel Landron on cul de sac Taitbout was built on the northern edge of what had been Louis XIII's wall. Hôtel Langeac on the Champs Elysees was built on the western edge of this barrier. Construction on Hôtel Langeac began in 1768 and was completed around 1780. Jefferson relocated there on 17 October 1785. He maintained his residence there until departing for home on 28 September 1789.

While vacant fields were being filled with neighborhoods on the outskirts of Quartiers du Palais Royal, Montmartre, and Saint Denis, several impressive projects were begun and completed in the center of Paris. The most significant of these were in the precincts near the king's city residence.

First among these was the Place de Louis XV at the western end of the Tuileries Garden. Approval had been secured in 1748 to create an equestrian statue of the aging King. His Highness donated a parcel of land a few years later. In 1757, royal architect Jacques-Ange Gabriel drew the plan for a plaza. After numerous delays, it finally opened with the statue of Louis XV at its center in 1775. This park completed an elaborate western entrance into heart of the city by linking the Champs Elysees with the Tuileries Garden and Palace.

As Gabriel was drawing his plan for la Place de Louis XV, the king commissioned him to design a pair of buildings to adorn its northern perimeter. Alexandre-Jean Noël pictured these two striking neo-classical structures in his 1772 portrait of the park. The building on the left became the residence of the duc de Aumont, who soon sold it to architect Louis-François Trouard. In this building on 6 February 1778, Benjamin Franklin, John Adams, and Silas Deane signed the treaty in which France recognized the United States and formalized their relations. The building on its right is the Hôtel de la Marine, which from its beginning provided offices for the French Navy. The avenue between them, rue Royale, links Gabriel's plaza to the Church of Saint Marie-Madeleine, which was completed a few years after the plaza.

A second notable project was undertaken by the king's distant cousin, Joseph Louis-Philippe, 6th duc d'Orleans. The duc inherited his title and the Palais Royal from his father in 1780. The following year he began to renovate and expand it. This work was in its final stages when Jefferson took up his brief residence there in August of 1784.

The duc's regal home faced the Louvre from across rue Saint-Honoré. His garden filled the block behind his palace. The addition he added consisted of an inner ring of buildings around this garden. When finished, its three four-storied arcades housed 145 cafes, shops, clubs, and theatres. One of the duc's first tenants was Dr. Philippe Curtius who leased two spaces in galerie de Montpensier to house his wax works. In the galerie de Valois, which enclosed the north end of the garden, aviator Pilâtre de Rosier opened the world's first museum of flight, which he called the Musée du Comte d'Artois in honor of its sponsor. Jefferson patronized both establishments.

A timbered pavilion known as le Camp des Tartares separated the garden from the duc's residence. This notorious mall featured an array of lewd spectacles and salacious exhibits that lured voyeurs from across Parisian society. Among the popular attractions were Mademoiselle Lapierre, a bearded Prussian woman who stood seven feet tall, and Labelle Zulima, a wax effigy of a nude woman that passers by were free to ogle. For the payment of a few sous, the more inquisitive could lift the veil that covered her lower extremities and explore the charms hidden there. They could continue their investigations in the upper floors of the other galleries, where bevies of prostitutes received visitors.

The disreputable behavior encouraged by the Barbarian's Camp was not the emporium's only idiosyncrasy. The duc, who had become the focal point of opposition to the monarchy at the time of Louis XVI's coronation, quietly encouraged disaffected philosophes from the city's teeming lower classes to gather under his roofs. By the time of Jefferson's arrival, the Palais Royal had become a center for political intrigue and sedition. Strolling through its arcades, Jefferson would have heard a stream of political harangues. He probably perused more than one handbill denouncing the monarchy and demanding its replacement. France's revolution would start with such a harangue in front of the Café du Foy (in the far corner of the galerie de Montpensier) a few weeks before Jefferson's departure.

A third project that bears mention was the grain warehouse where Jefferson met Maria Cosway in August of 1786. La Halle aux Blés was the largest structure in the produce marketing section east of the Palais Royal. It was built between 1763 and 1767. Its dome, which Jefferson admired, was added in 1782. This market area was one of the few places in the city where upper crusts from the western suburbs interacted with tradesmen and laborers from the city's proletarian eastern quartiers.

Before he visited la Halle aux Blés, Jefferson made two excursions into the city's northeastern sector. The first of these took place a month after Jefferson moved to Hôtel Landron. On this occasion, Jefferson attended an art auction conducted by a Monsieur Paillet. Monsieur Paillet's gallery appears to have been one of several in a sprawling mansion built in the late-1620s by Claude de Bullion, Minister of Finance under Louis XIII. Hôtel Bullion was a block north of la Halle aux Blés on rue Platriere. This street was later renamed rue Jean-Jacques Rousseau in honor of the *philosophe* who lived there between 1770 and 1778. Jefferson bought two paintings from M. Paillet.

Jefferson attended a second art auction in February of 1785. This outing took him to within a block or two of the Bastille. His destination was the former home of "deceased collector" Dupille de Saint-Severin on rue Saint Louis. Jefferson bought five paintings at this auction. Whether he paused to inspect the nearby fortress is not known.

This quarter of the city had been fashionable when Bullion and Saint-Severin built their mansions. Henry IV had attracted such wealthy peers by settling the city's first public square, la Place Royale, in the heart of its Marais district. Several grand maisons were built on and near this plaza. Among these were the Hôtel de Sens, the Hôtel de Sully, the Hôtel de Beauvais, and the Hôtel de Guénégauds. The Hôtel de Carnavalet was built during the 16th century. During the sector's 17th century salad days, it became the home of cele-brated letter writer, the marquise de Sévigné. In 1866 the city of Paris transformed her home into the Musée de Carnavalet, which continues to conserve the art and history of Paris.

The Bastille was a block to the east of le Place Royale. Built in earlier centuries, Charles V transformed it into the city's fortified eastern gate in the 1300s. Beyond this gate lay Faubourg Saint Antoine. In Jefferson's time, tourists did not venture into it unless they had "a particular interest in manufacturing." It seems Jefferson did not. Bakeries, furniture shops, and other manufactories were attracted to this drab suburb by tax exemptions and other regulatory measures devised to draw industry to the city. By the time Jefferson reached Paris, the artisans and laborers who operated these enter-prises had replaced the idle rich who brightened the city's northeastern quadrant in the pervious century. The city's Jewish community was also there, at the center of what had once been a swamp.

One 18th century courtier who bucked the trend to locate in Quartier du Saint Germain des Pres in the city's southwestern corner was Pierre Augustin Caron de Beaumarchais. During the American Revolution, Beaumarchais conducted the clandestine business of Roderigue Hortalez and Company from the library of his hôtel at 47 rue Vielle du Temple. In 1787, he purchased an acre of inexpensive real estate between le Place Royale and the Bastille. On it, he built one of the grandest villas in Paris. Jefferson attended a performance of Beaumarchais' celebrated comedy. He also received a visit from the man his country refused to pay for the arms that turned the tide of the American Revolution. Whether Jefferson ever visited the playwright-turned-arms dealer's spectacular home is not known.

The southeastern sector of Jefferson's Paris featured a number of distinguished public and philanthropic institutions. The Hall of Wine still overlooks the Seine opposite Ile Saint Louis. Beside it are the King's Gardens. Jefferson had reasons for visiting both places and is said to have been "a frequent visitor to the Jardin du Roi." To the east of the gardens was la Hospice de la Salpêtrière, which began its long life as a gunpowder factory in the 16th century. In the mid-17th century, Louis XIII converted it into a repository for the poor. In the next century, Louis XIV added to its functions that of a prison for prostitutes and as an asylum for the mentally ill and criminally insane. When Jefferson reached Paris, this "hospital" is said to have had 10,000 patients. There is no record that Jefferson visited it.

A far grander institution, one that Jefferson did visit, was named after the patron saint of Paris. Planning for the Church of Saint Genevieve began in 1755. Two years later, Jacques-Germain Soufflot completed his astonishing plan for a church that could be seen from every point in the city. Construction was still in progress when Jefferson inspected it (date unknown). The revolution had begun by the time the work was completed in 1790. Soufflet's masterpiece was then seized and put to use as a secular mausoleum for the city's greatest sons. Among the remains interred there are those of Voltaire and Rousseau. The body of Jefferson's friend Pierre Cabanis was also interred there, but his heart was buried in the garden of Madame Helvétius's estate in Auteuil.

Next to the Church of Saint Genevieve was one of the city's most treasured institutions. The colleges of the University of Paris spread through the neighborhoods north of Soufflot's awe-inspiring landmark. In earlier times, instruction at the Sorbonne and the university's other colleges was conducted in Latin, hence the name Latin Quarter, which is still used to identify this section of Paris.

The city's southwestern sector was mostly open ground at the beginning of the 18th century. Much of its land was owned by the Princes Condé who inherited their title from the uncle of Bourbon King Henry IV. In the decade before Jefferson reached France, the reigning Prince began to develop the grounds of Hôtel de Condé. La Théâtre-Français was the flagship structure in this development. Built between 1779 and 1782 in the garden of his hôtel, it featured the Palladian design of Charles De Wailly and his schoolmate, Marie-Joseph Peyre. Jefferson attended five performances at this theatre, including *The Marriage of Figaro,* which he saw on August 4, 1786.

Behind the theatre, across rue de Vaugirard, is the Palais du Luxembourg. The palace and its garden complex were built in the mid-1600s as a residence for Louis XIII's mother, Marie de' Medici. In 1750, its galleries were opened two days a week for public viewing. This policy appears to have ended after Louis XVI gifted the property to his brother, the comte de Provence, which he did in 1778. There is no record that Jefferson visited the palace or its ground, but given the number of performances he attended across the street, it seems likely that he at least toured the palace's magnificent gardens.

L'Hôtel national des Invalides was built for Louis XIV in the last decades of the 17th century to provide a hospital and home for the veterans of his many wars. Its dome was completed in 1708. No record shows that Jefferson visited it.

As the 18th century wore on, this quarter of Paris grew more appealing to aristocrats obliged to accompany the king to and from Versailles. The Palais de Bourbon was among the first of their magnificent structures. Completed in 1728, it was the residence of Louise Françoise de Bourbon, duchesse de Bourbon. The duchesse was the daughter of Louis XIV and his mistress, marquise of Montespan. The marquis de Lafayette's townhome was on rue de Bourbon a few blocks to its east. A few blocks further east, on rue de Seine, was Hôtel la Rochefoucauld. Jefferson went there often to commune with the duc and his thoughtful mother, duchesse d'Anville.

Adjacent to the duc de la Rochefoucauld's residence was le Hôtel de Monnaies, which housed the royal Mint. The building was completed in 1773. The following year, the marquis de Condorcet, having become Inspector General of the Mint, moved into one of its apartments. Midway between the Palais de Bourbon and the Hôtel de Monnaies was the Hôtel de Salm. Construction on this mesmerizing building began in 1782 and finished under Jefferson's watchful eye five years later. A few blocks south of this structure, on rue de Grenelle, was the Abbaye royale de Panthemont. The church and the school Jefferson's daughters attended there had been rebuilt and expanded in the 1740s.

Early in the 13th century, Phillipe Auguste placed the first pavers on streets in Paris. A few of these streets reportedly had drains that conveyed collected fluids into the Seine. Over the next six centuries, the city expanded much faster than its drainage system. In Jefferson's time, Parisian streets had gutters that ran along at their centers. Lacking drains, filth—including human waste—lingered in these troughs even through dry weather. The stench was by all accounts awful. Since few streets had sidewalks, pedestrians faced the hazard of being sprayed when carriages raced by. Foot travelers might also be run over. Injury and death from such accidents were commonplace in Jefferson's time.

Louis XIV's improvement projects included expanding his capital's primitive sewer system. Under his direction, a tunneled circuit was built beneath the faubourgs on the right bank of the Seine. This circuit emptied into the river between Pont au Change and Pont Notre Dame across from Ile de la Cite. A similar circuit was built south of the river. This circuit drained into Riviere Biévre, which emptied into the Seine between the King's Garden and the Hospital de la Salpêtrière. Besides the sewage and run off, le Manufacture des Gobelins and the area's tanning factories poured pollutants into this poor creek. It must have been the most poisonous waterway in the world. There is no record that Jefferson inspected this unnatural wonder. He did frequently cross the Seine, however, which must have been just as polluted. When he did, he would have seen some of the 2000 washerwomen who made their livings pounding clothes "clean" in its tainted water.

During his first weeks in Paris, Jefferson avoided the city's filth by staying near his lodgings. Philippe Mazzei claimed that Jefferson brought a phaeton with him from Virginia. Traveling by horse-drawn vehicle would have helped him to avoid being soiled. About the time he signed his lease for the Hôtel Landron, he reportedly purchased "a handsome carriage with green morocco lining that put the old phaeton to shame." [Lawrence S. Kaplan. *Thomas Jefferson: Westward the Course of Empire.* Rowman & Littlefield. 1998. 211.] Where Jefferson kept these vehicles and the horses he needed to convey them during his first year in Paris is not clear. This uncertainty resolved when he moved to Hôtel Langeac, which, unlike Hôtel Landron, had a spacious garden and stables.

Jefferson had several reasons to move to this elegant mansion. It was better suited for entertaining. It placed him nearer to the Court at Versailles. And it had the stables he needed to maintain his conveyances. But also, Jefferson went to France to mingle with the best and brightest people. Living in this stylish mansion on the Champs Elysees allowed him to do this while avoiding the filth, the stench, and the meaner sorts who filled the French capital.

chapter six

The French Enlightenment – The Idea Men

*I*n the mid-18th century, a doctrinaire French encyclopedist set out to teach the people of France "what is true and what is false." As Diderot began to do this, a scholar at the Sorbonne unveiled a new interpretation of human history. According to Anne Robert Jacques Turgot, all problems of society can be solved through the application of knowledge, and as they are, mankind will advance to a state of perfection.

Turgot devoted his life to implementing this idea, rising in 1774 to become chief financial officer of France. His protégé and biographer, Marie Jean Antoine Nicolas de Caritat, marquis de Condorcet, redefined his mentor's concept into a "law of nature," that is referred to today as the Doctrine of Progress. By the time Jefferson reached Paris in the summer of 1784, these men and these ideas had transformed the Enlightenment in France into a reform movement that Jefferson joined in 1787.

Neither Jefferson nor the patriots who organized and managed the war for American independence were like Diderot, or Turgot, or their colleagues. These Americans were not spreading truth or perfecting society. They were lawyers, legislators, and provocateurs who wanted the power to define the common good of the American people and to make the laws to accomplish it. They knew little if anything about the Enlightenment in France, or the reform movement it produced.

During the fifty years before Jefferson reached Paris, a handful of irreverent insurgents launched a series of intellectual revolutions that together constituted the French Enlightenment. They modernized the Natural Sciences. They invented a new Science of Government. They invented a new Science of Man and conceptualized a new Morality. They introduced new forms of Arts and Letters. They separated Man from God and bridled the authority of the Catholic Church.

As these insurgencies took root and spread, the people of France came to understand that the problems afflicting their society were insufferable. The monarchy was bankrupt. Corruption was everywhere. The economy was stagnant. There was no justice. And millions of peasants were starving in the countryside.

I believe Jefferson became aware of these things during conversations with his reform-minded friends. In my earlier work, I conducted these conversations between Jefferson and his French friend, Pierre Cabanis. In respect to the enlightened trends in French thought, Cabanis was arguably the best-informed man in France.

Cabanis used his training in Medicine to become a pioneer in the field of Physiology. He became a *philosophe* under the watchful eyes of Turgot and Condorcet and by studying the Science of Man espoused by his patron's deceased husband, Claude Helvétius. As a *philosophe,* he embraced Reason over Faith as the lens for viewing the world. He moved his residence to the Auteuil estate of Madame Helvétius in the summer of 1778. He became her doctor and companion and an intimate friend of "Papa" Franklin. He attended the gatherings she hosted for scientists, philosophers, and Freemasons, and deliberated with them on how to fix the problems that afflicted France's government and society. These connections allowed Cabanis to build a unique network of associations across Parisian society.

Franklin inducted him into the Lodge of the Nine Sisters a few months after he initiated Voltaire, which he did in April 1778. Freemasonry, with its creed of social virtue, benevolence, and self-improvement, provided a valuable system of support for Cabanis in his later work modernizing the hospital system of the French capital and as a medical researcher.

In *Thomas Jefferson's Enlightenment,* I put readers in the company of Cabanis and Jefferson. We join them on eight excursions in which Cabanis shows his American companion selected sites in the French capital. As he does, he weaves the threads of the French Enlightenment into the concept of Progress. The cognoscenti Cabanis introduces Jefferson to are no longer seekers of truth. They are progressive reformers. Benjamin Franklin has taught them to see America as the glistening city on the hill and "government by the people" as the destination of the great march of human progress.

We are with Jefferson when he meets the duc de la Rochefoucauld. The duc is the leader of an influential group that favors replacing the decrepit French monarchy with a constitutional government based on a properly formed bill of rights. The author of the *Declaration of Independence* soon becomes an integral part of their plan to reform France.

The Idea Men Who Enlightened France

François-Marie Arouet, better known as **Voltaire,** has been described as the Godfather of the Enlightenment in France. The intellectual revolutions that comprised it began five years after he returned from a three-year self-imposed exile to England in 1729 when he published his *Lettres Philosophiques.* In these letters, Voltaire endorsed the empirical method of Isaac Newton and the modernization in learning espoused by Francis Bacon. He also recommended the materialist philosophy of John Locke. Each of these innovative thinkers, Voltaire advised, contributed to the concept of Liberty that underpinned England's constitutional system. With his seminal work, the impudent satirist emerged as an insightful social critic.

Voltaire inspired a few determined admirers to undertake initiatives of their own. In his conversation piece, *La Sainte Cène du Patriarche* (c.1772), Jean Huber pictures the aged sage passing the baton to the rising generation of opinion managers. Seated around him at table are Baron Grimm, d'Alembert and La Harpe, Sophie d'Houdetot, the poet Saint-Lambert, Diderot, Marmontel, and Condorcet. While entertaining and informing France's educated professional class (its clerisy), Voltaire had invented *public opinion*. By the time of his death in 1778, he had persuaded France's clerisy to support the reforms his followers were advocating.

Denis Diderot carried Voltaire's revolution into the Arts and Religion. He is remembered today for his *Encyclopaedia, or a Systematic Dictionary of the Sciences, Arts, and Crafts.* "An encyclopedia," Diderot explained, "should encompass not only the fields already covered by the academies, but each and every branch of human knowledge." He confirmed that he was following Voltaire by dedicating his work to Bacon, Locke, and Newton.

For Diderot, Reason was less a tool for advancing knowledge than a ram to batter down the habitually dark dwelling place in which mankind lived. In his great instauration, Bacon undertook to change the way men perceived the world. Diderot undertook to change the way *other* men perceived it. To do this, he commissioned dozens of the most brilliant and knowledgeable men of his age to write what came to be 71,818 articles, which he published between 1751 and 1772 in a set of 28 volumes. Contributors included Voltaire (History, Literature, Philosophy), Rousseau (Music, Social Theory), Turgot (Economics and Philosophical Topics), d'Alembert (Co-editor and Scientific Topics), Montesquieu (on "Taste"), and Quesnay (Economic Topics). In his frontispiece illustration, Charles-Nicolas Cochin characterized their collected contributions as the "Truth". Diderot pursued it with the understanding that it would activate "the power to change men's common way of thinking." Everyone was to benefit.

Jean-Jacques Rousseau was arguably the most influential thinker of the French Enlightenment. He was also its most vocal opponent. His philosophy also underpinned the reform movement Thomas Jefferson joined and inspired the insurgents who overthrew the French monarchy. Most members of the people's committee that seized control of the first French republic and initiated the bloody Reign of Terror in 1793 were Rousseau's followers.

Diderot met Rousseau in 1742. Rousseau established himself as an authority on man and society eight years later by explicating a position Diderot suggested in jest. (Diderot is said to have advised his friend to submit a competitive essay denying that the revival in France's arts and sciences had improved French manners or morals.) During the first seven years of the *Encyclopedie*, Diderot printed several articles by Rousseau. Their friendship—and Rousseau's association with Diderot's progressive circle—ended with a famous quarrel in 1758. Temperamental differences had made theirs a tension-filled relationship. The final break occurred after Diderot made damaging comments about Rousseau's one-sided love affair with Sophie d'Houdetot. Rousseau publically denounced Diderot and disparaged his pedagogical mission and method in his hundred-page *Lettre à M. d'Alembert*.

Rousseau built his reputation on the claim that man, by nature a noble savage, enslaved and corrupted himself by joining society. He opened his argument for social equality in his 1754 essay *Discourse on the Origin and Foundation of Inequality* with the claim that "the fruits of the earth belong to us all and the earth itself to nobody." In his back-to-nature social theology, Rousseau blamed industry and the accumulation of property for setting one man against another and making them unequal. "In proportion as they grew enlightened," he announced, "they grew industrious . . . they invented several kinds of implements of hard and sharp stones, then made huts out of branches, and afterwards learnt to plaster them over with mud and clay. This was the epoch of a first revolution, which established and distinguished families, and introduced a kind of property, in itself the source of a thousand quarrels and conflicts . . ."

Rousseau eventually revised his position, arguing that society should rest on a social contract, which activates the *general will* of the people. He went on to claim that the exercise of this general will would necessarily promote liberty, equality, and fraternity. All society's problems would resolve, Rousseau theorized, if the people were able to implement it. In Rousseau's anti-enlightened theory, science had little to do with achieving the common good. While his former colleagues in the encyclopedia movement heralded advances in learning and technology as the way to achieve a state of perfection, Rousseau advocated simplicity and commonality of values.

Anne Robert Jacques Turgot was the only *philosophe* of the French Enlightenment to apply his knowledge as a social reformer. He established himself as a theorist while studying theology at the

Sorbonne (1749–1750). His unanimous election as Prior of the Society of the Sorbonne obliged him to present two discourses in 1750. He titled the second of these "A Philosophical Review of the Successive Advances of the Human Mind." In this lecture, Stephen Walker observed in his 1895 biography, Turgot argued that "society was capable of enjoying greatly improved conditions, and that, step by step, stage by stage, century by century, these conditions might be still further improved."

Walker characterized Turgot's analysis as "the earliest enunciation of the doctrine of the perfectibility of the human race." The essence of his position was that advances in scientific knowledge and in the arts impact society in ways that are constructive and cumulative. As they improve quality of life for society's members, they lead mankind toward a state of increasing perfection.

Shortly after delivering this celebrated lecture, Turgot abandoned his plan to enter the Church and instead entered public service. Leaving his studies with a new understanding of his life's mission, he accepted the post of Deputy Councillor of the Procurator-General in Paris. Two years later, he became a Councillor in the Parliament of Paris. The following year, he accepted appointment as Master of Requests. Turgot held this position until 1761 when he was named Intendant of the Limousin district, one of the poorest regions of France. He took up residence in its capital, Limoges, where he remained for thirteen years, laboring to stimulate economic growth. He undertook to do this by implementing policies advocated by a group of *laissez-faire* economists who called themselves Physiocrats.

Turgot's success in Limousin attracted the attention of France's new king. In 1774, Louis XVI named him his chief financial officer. As Comptroller General of France, Turgot endeavored to re-establish the "government of nature" by eliminating regulations and taxes that obstructed the free flow of goods to market.

By the time Jefferson reached France, its best men and women had adopted Turgot's optimistic view of human history and were exploring how to apply scientific knowledge to advance the great march of human progress.

The father of **Claude Adrien Helvétius** was first physician to Marie Leszczyńska, wife of French King Louis XV. Son Claude acquired his own fortune as a Farmer General collecting the king's taxes. In 1751, he married the niece of famed hostess Madame de Graffigny. He reportedly took his beautiful wife to his estate southeast of Paris to mitigate the danger of her seduction. At Château de Voré au Perche, with encouragement from his faithful wife, Helvétius dedicated himself to Philosophy. Over the next seven years, he created the work for which he is remembered. His lack of training helps to explain the originality of *De l'esprit (On Mind)*.

The late-blooming *philosophe* built his new Science of Man on the materialist theory of mind John Locke unveiled in his *Essay Concerning Human Understanding*. Physical sensitivity, Helvétius argued, is the causal source of all mental activity. Even the capacity to manipulate ideas—intelligence—was a product of eternal sensations. Helvétius's claim that aptitude was not a natural quality enraged aristocrats in France whose superiority and hereditary privileges rested on the higher quality of their blood.

Helvétius's materialism led him to other controversial positions. He concluded, for example, that the fundamental law of human behavior is the search for pleasurable sensations. More shocking was his claim that the well-being of the community is the standard for right behavior: acts of individuals are morally acceptable so far as they contribute to the common good and morally unacceptable to the extent they diminish it. France's clergy were appalled by this claim since it separated morality from God's divine Will—and their interpretation of it.

Helvétius suggested that even the lowest members of society could be taught to behave in ways that were conducive to its well-being. This could be done, he said, by reinforcing their instruction with pleasurable sensations. With this novel idea, Helvétius made pleasure an essential component of societal reform. Progressives during Jefferson's time in Paris accepted that training the people to find pleasure in socially constructive ways was vital for perfecting their society. This was a prominent theme in the salon hosted by Madame d'Houdetot, which Jefferson probably attended on occasion.

David Hume called Helvétius's idea *utility*. During the late-18th century and through the 19th century, Adam Smith, Jeremy Bentham, J.S. Mill, and their followers became forceful proponents of a concept of utilitarianism that had its roots in Helvétius's Science of Man.

The accomplishments of Marie Jean Antoine Nicolas de Caritat, **Marquis de Condorcet,** were innumerable, but his most enduring achievement was his distillation of Turgot's theory into a Law of Nature.

Like his mentor, Condorcet believed that the ever-expanding library of human knowledge contained solutions for every problem of man in society. He also believed that as men apply their expanding knowledge to resolve society's afflictions, society would achieve an ever-increasing state of perfection. According to his Doctrine of Progress, the advance from barbarism toward refinement is inevitable and unlimited.

This powerful principle confirmed that the intellectual revolutions of the French Enlightenment were naturally constructive and beneficial to society. In formalizing this idea, Condorcet, whose own life ended tragically during the Reign of Terror, cemented the optimism of the society Jefferson joined in pre-revolutionary France.

A great French *philosophe* established Progress as the Law of Nature. A village sage from America, **Benjamin Franklin,** identified its destination.

Franklin's reputation was established in France in 1752. That was the year King Louis XV read comte de Buffon's comments on the Pennsylvanian's experiment with electricity. The king requested that it be reproduced in his presence and was delighted by the result. Afterwards, he sent the scientist who discovered the unknown force of nature a complimentary letter.

Franklin traveled from London to Paris in August of 1767. In his five weeks there, Franklin met the King and Queen. His purpose for going, however, was to discuss his views on taxation and related matters with a group of physiocratic economists. Among the men he conferred with on this occasion were comte de Maribeau, du Pont de Nemours, Doctor Jacques Dubourg, and translator Thomas-François Dalibard. He may also have met Turgot.

Franklin returned to France two years later for what appears to have been a month-long vacation. Although there is no record of it, he probably met again with Dubourg to discuss Dubourg's idea for translating Franklin's works into French. (Dubourg made and directed the translation of "Franklin's complete works" and published them in the two-volume *Oeuvres de M. Franklin* in September 1773.) Dubourg's translations were revised and reissued in 1777. This second edition attracted the interest of the French people and made the American "homespun" a hero in their eyes. Prior to publication of the first edition, in August of 1772, Franklin received the honor of being elected a member of the French Academy of Sciences.

Long admired as a scientist and inventor and as a philosopher and a man of letters, when Franklin arrived Paris in late-December 1776, he became a sought after spokesman for the American cause. He was immediately besieged by enthusiastic young *Americanistes* seeking commissions in George Washington's American army.

Desperate to repulse the invasion by England's armies, the American Congress had dispatched Franklin to France to solicit military and financial support. But when he arrived, he discovered that neither the king nor his Foreign Minister would meet with him. The king was of course a monarchist and did not wish to insinuate that he supported either Republicanism or a republican state. His Foreign Minister, Charles Gravier, compte de Vergennes did not want to antagonize England, with whom France was keeping a fragile peace.

Franklin waited two weeks at the Hôtel d'Entragues on rue de l'Université in Faubourg de Saint Germain. Besieged by office seekers, he moved three times before receiving an invitation from Jacques-Donatien le Ray de Chaumont to take an apartment in a guesthouse on his estate. Franklin accepted this invitation and, in March of 1777, he moved to his final French residence at l'hôtel de Valentinois in Passy.

Franklin appears to have made his debut into French society prior to relocating to Passy. The occasion was one of Madame du Deffand's Monday evening salons. If Franklin did not encounter the duc de la Rochefoucauld at this time, he did so soon afterwards. (Franklin may have met the duc in London during one of the duc's visits there in the late-1760s.) By the winter of 1777, La Rochefoucauld had made the first French translation of the *Declaration of Independence.* A second translation may have "been completed with the allegedly eager assistance of Benjamin Franklin." An enthusiastic admirer of America and a champion of the American cause, the duc became a key figure in Franklin's program to win French support for the American war effort.

If Franklin met Turgot during his 1767 vacation to Paris, the duc reintroduced him to Franklin at this time. Franklin probably also met Lafayette at this time. The young major general would soon depart for America on a ship he purchased himself to transport his baggage and his staff. Franklin's colleague, Silas Deane, had arranged the appointment, but manners and protocol would have required an interview with the American diplomat before Lafayette embarked on his famous adventure. He sailed for America on 20 April 1777.

Through the remaining months of that year, Franklin waited for the diplomatic ice to thaw. As he did, he negotiated loans, dined with cognoscenti, and fended off commission seekers. While doing these things, Franklin reinforced France's favorable opinion of America and its enlightened pursuit of Liberty. He built this campaign around an image of himself as the quintessential American—a homespun in a beaver skin hat. An image of "fur hat Franklin" was drawn by the same artist who designed the frontispiece for Diderot's *Encyclopedie*. Not long before C.N. Cochin created this famous piece of propaganda, he drew a commonly reproduced image of Turgot.

Cochin's engraving was selling like hotcakes in Paris when the shocking news arrived that General Burgoyne had surrendered his army. This opened the door for a new Franco–American relationship. The following month, on 6 January 1778, French diplomat Conrad Alexandre Gérard de Rayneval signed a Treaty of Alliance and a Treaty of Amity and Commerce. Franklin, Adams, and Silas Deane signed it on behalf of America.

Later in that summer, Turgot escorted Franklin to the home of Turgot's one-time inamorata, Anne-Catherine de Ligniville, Madame Helvétius. Madame was Franklin's neighbor and lived within walking distance of his lodgings. The American homespun dined with her and her companion every week. Before returning to America in 1785, Franklin is said to have proposed marriage. La Notre Dame d'Auteuil graciously declined.

The treaties Franklin signed opened the floodgate for French aid. It proved decisive in the campaigns of 1779 and 1780. Negotiations for peace began after a French-American army forced Cornwallis to surrender in October of 1781. By then, the salons of the Golden Age were gone. The salons that took their places were hosted by Franklin's admirers, including Madame Helvétius, Madame d'Houdetot, and duchesse d'Anville, the mother of duc de la Rochefoucauld. Their gatherings provided forums where enlightened progressives deliberated on how to reform France. Franklin spent his last five-year in France encouraging these lumieres to see America as the fulfillment of their progressive vision. Turgot reinforced this idea in the epigram he wrote to honor Franklin: "He seized the lightning from the sky, and the scepter from tyrants". By then the homeland of the village sage, built on Liberty and the Rights of Man, was recognized as the embodiment of the new world order.

chapter seven

Freemasonry: A Force for Social Progress

$\mathcal{T}$he Masonic creed — *Public Virtue, Benevolence, Self Betterment* — was an expression of the enlightened impulse that propelled events in France during the decades leading up to the French Revolution. "Fellowcraft" therefore attracted France's best and most able men. As many as half the men Jefferson associated with in French were Freemasons. They were progressives and leaders in the movement to reform France during the years preceding its bloody revolution.

French Freemasons did not see their fraternity as a social organization. They saw it as the *Royal Art,* a vessel that conveyed timeless truths about the way men should conduct their lives. Learned brothers in France's thinking class applied them as they replaced Aristotelian formalism with modern methods of science and as they replaced religion-based commands with the instruction of Reason in matters of right behavior. Civic-minded brothers in France's privileged classes practiced it by organizing benevolent associations and by pressing for social reform. Brothers in France's educated lower classes applied it by striving to improve themselves.

The France Jefferson visited in the late-1780s was a century behind England in respect to the state of its society. In England, an agricultural revolution had begun early in the 17th century. An industrial revolution had begun early in the 18th century. By the time Jefferson reached France, new agricultural and industrial technologies were leveling England's manor-based hierarchy and ending its thousand-year history as an agrarian economy. When Jefferson reached Paris, England was a dynamic, increasingly integrated, commercial system that rewarded innovation and personal industry.

When Jefferson arrived, France's best men were contemplating how to duplicate England's success. In this connection, Freemasonry served as an invaluable resource by facilitating the flow of ideas and technical innovation that was necessary to modernize France's agrarian economy and bring the country into the modern world of commerce.

As cosmopolitans on France's high plateau pondered these complex matters, middling sorts launched their own deliberations and began to formulate their own plans. Leaders in these low level discussions were also Freemasons. Inspired by the American Revolution, they seized upon the ideas that they, too, had rights by Nature, and that it was their right to alter or abolish their government that impeded their pursuit of happiness.

When Jefferson arrived in France, Freemasons in the political clubs of Paris were laying the foundations for a new society with a government by the people. It would be based on the rights Rousseau claimed for all men. Guiding their budding movement to change and modernize the French government was the Masonic-like creed of *Liberty, Equality, Fraternity.*

Those who have built their knowledge of Thomas Jefferson with information provided by his 20th century biographers, Dumas Malone for example, do not know that Freemasonry was a leading force in the change that occurred in 18th century France. Nor do they know that Jefferson spent most of his time communing with Freemasons and their friends.

First among these was his revolutionary-era cohort, Benjamin Franklin. Franklin became a Freemason in Philadelphia in 1731. In the spring of 1778 he began the first of his two terms as Venerated Master of the Parisian Lodge of the Nine Sisters. It was his honor to lead the initiation of Voltaire into the Craft, which he did in the month before the celebrated *littérature's* demise. Other American practitioners of the Craft were Colonel David Humphrey, secretary of the American delegation in Paris; Jefferson's personal secretary, William Short; and naval hero John Paul Jones. Short and Jones joined Franklin's lodge after Franklin assumed his post as its venerated master.

The Lodge of the Nine Sisters is perhaps the most famous of France's revolutionary era lodges because of Franklin and Voltaire. It was founded in 1776 by Joseph Jérôme Lefrançois de Lalande. In addition to his high standing as a scientist (Astronomy), Lalande had been a close friend of fellow Mason Claude Adrian Helvétius. At the time of Helvétius's death, the two men had been planning to form a "Masonic learned society" where scientists could exchange information and share their enlightened thoughts. Helvétius's loving widow was instrumental in making her deceased husband's dream a reality.

In addition to Franklin, Voltaire, Short, and Jones, members of this lodge included many important French intellectuals. Among these were economist abbé Sieyès, Dr. Guillotin, the sculptor Houdin, and naturalist comte de Lacépède. The younger members of Madame Helvétius's entourage all affiliated with this lodge. These included Pierre Cabanis, Destutt d'Tracy, Nicolas Chamfort, Dominique Joseph Garat, and Constantin Volney. Jefferson formed enduring friendships with Cabanis, Tracy, and Volney.

La Loge de Contrat Social [The Lodge of the Social Contract] adopted the fellowcraft of the Scottish Rite. Perhaps because the Scottish Rite embraces the idea that Freemasons belong to a brotherhood and are themselves an order of knights, it attracted members of the French military, including several officers who served in the American Revolution. Among these were the marquis de Lafayette, vicomte de Rochambeau, his aide count de Ségur, count Chambrun (Lafayette's cousin), Andre Boniface Louis Riqueti, vicomte de Mirabeau (whose brother authored a passionate attack on the Society of the Cincinnati and was known by Jefferson), viscount de Ricce (aide de camp to M. la baron de Viomenil who commanded the assault on Redoubt 9 at Yorktown), and the marquis de Casteras (who distinguished himself in Savannah under count d'Estaing).

A third notable Parisian lodge was La Loge des Amis Reunis [The Lodge of the People Together]. Charles Pierre-Paul, marquis de Savalette de Langes, founded this lodge in 1771. Savalette was the son of Charles Pierre Savalette de Magnanville. The father was the senior of two Gardes du Trésor royal (Keepers of the Royal Treasury). In 1773, his son became the junior Keeper of the Royal Treasury. Because so many members of this lodge were financiers, it was referred to as the home of les Crésus de la Maçonnerie (the wealthy ones among the Masons).

Members of this lodge advanced through twelve "orders", the highest being la Philalethes, the seekers of truth. Members of this lofty circle had ties to an esoteric sect known as the Bavarian Illuminati, whose two-fold mission was to teach people how to be happy and help them achieve it by freeing themselves from the shackles of religious superstition. In keeping with this enlightened vision, la Loge Amis Reunis embraced a social philosophy based on equality. One of its tenets was the abolition of the privileges that accompanied social rank.

The lodge's elite members tended to be tepid supporters of this ideal. One member who seemed to embrace it was Louis Alexandre, duc de la Rochefoucauld-Anville. His cousin, François Alexandre Frédéric, duc de La Rochefoucauld-Liancourt, also affiliated with this lodge as did the duc de Biron, and the marquis du Condorcet, whose initiation into the brotherhood has never been confirmed. These men were joined by baron d'Allarde, viscount de Beauharnis, vicomte de Tavannes, Dutrousett d'Hericourt (who was President of the Parliament of Paris), and the brothers La Meth (who saw action at Yorktown). Comte de Roederer (friend of Madame Helvétius) and du Pont de Nemours were also affiliated with this lodge.

Support for social equality was more energetic among the lodge's "new" men—those who had to earn their livings. These included minor clergy, lawyers, doctors, and entrepreneurs. Many were writers. Among its clergy were abbé Gregoire and abbé d'Espagnac. Its lawyers included Isaac René Guy Le Chaplier and Maximilien Robespierre, both of whom were disciples of Rousseau. Antoine Barnave, Georges Jacques Danton, and Adrien Duport trained in the law, but found their calling in politics.

Besides writing many successful plays, including the scandalous Figaro trilogy, Pierre-Augustin Caron de Beaumarchais supplied arms to the American army during the American Revolution. His first shipments arrived in time to turn the tide in favor of the Americans at the critical Battle of Saratoga.

Nicolas Chamfort left Madame Helvétius's salon to join the household of the Prince of Condé. Marie Antoinette once teased him saying that, "you pleased all the world at Versailles not because of your talent, but in spite of it." Andre Chenier wrote poetry when he was not tending the affairs of Chevalier de la Luzerne's delegation in London. Count de Gebelin became famous by reading the future in Tarot cards. Choderlos de Laclos was secretary to the duc d'Orleans and the author of the provocative novel *Les liaisons dangereuses*. Louis-Sébastien Mercier was called Le Singe de Jean-Jacques (Jean-Jacques' Ape) because he followed Rousseau in denying that scientific knowledge produces human progress. Jean-Paul Marat was trained as a physician. Prior to the Revolution, Marat maintained a scientific laboratory that Benjamin Franklin occasionally visited. A physician, Antoine Fourcroy was chosen to succeed Pierre Macquer as lecturer in chemistry in comte de Buffon's college at the Jardin du Roi. He was later elected a member of France's Academy of Sciences. In addition to being the youngest member of La Loge des Amis Reunis, Louis Antoine Saint-Just proved to be its most ruthless.

Jefferson's Charlottesville neighbor, Philip Mazzei, was said to be a Freemason, but it is not known whether he affiliated with a particular lodge when he was in residence in Paris.

In the fall of 1785, Jefferson began his association with the duc de la Rochefoucauld's small circle of reformers. By the winter of 1786, he had established himself as a member of this select group. Its guiding light, the marquis de Condorcet, was said to be a Mason, but as I say his initiation has never been confirmed. Lafayette was a dedicated member of the fraternity. Others Jefferson met in the duc's conclaves included Chastellux, who was not a Mason, du Pont de Nemours, who was a zealous Mason, and Victor Riqueti, marquis de Mirabeau who was also a Mason.

Many buildings that Louis XV commissioned during his beautification program were designed and built by Freemasons. Jefferson's residence, Hôtel Langeac, was designed by Jean-François-Thérèse Chalgrin (1739–1811) who was a member of The Simple Hearts of the North Star Lodge of Paris. Claude Nicolas Ledoux, the architect of the Farmers General, designed the neoclassical pavilions for their tax barrier, many of which were destroyed during the Revolution. Freemason Nicolas Le Camus de Mézières designed *Le Halle aux Blés*. One of the "masonic" buildings Jefferson visited during his stay in Paris was *le Théâtre Français,* which was the collaborative work of Monsieurs Peyre and de Wailly. Another, *le Abbaye Sainte-Geneviève,* was designed and built by Jacques Germain Soufflot. *Le Palais de Bourbon* was the work of Bernard Poyet. Pierre Rousseau's *l'hôtel de Salm* is famous for holding America's first architect in thrall for hours at a time.

chapter eight

The French Mind

The world Jefferson entered when he reached France in early August 1784 was substantially different from the one he had departed from in early July. In view of the dissimilarities in their histories, their social orders, and the problems they faced, it is not surprising that the French way of thinking would be different from Jefferson's.

Jefferson's worldview formed during a turbulent decade that began with protests against the Stamp Act in March of 1765 and ended with the shot "heard round the world." The knowledge he gained during these years prepared him to draft what is arguably the most important political document ever written, which his did as a member of the Second Continental Congress in June of 1776. As Jefferson prepared himself to write the *Declaration of Independence,* his cohorts in the patriotic party were learning to marshal the weight of numbers to accomplish political change.

In France, the vast majority of the people were peasants who could neither read, nor write, nor reason. Nor did they have political rights or a voice in deciding matters that affected their lives. Thinking was done by closed circles of cosmopolitans who had no material contact with common people.

When Jefferson arrived, the French people existed in three Estates. Each had its own thin upper crust and an impoverished mass below. The Clergy formed the First Estate. It contained approximately 125,000 members in Jefferson's time. The Aristocracy formed the Second Estate. It contained approximately 200,000 members in Jefferson's time. The Commons contained the remainder of France's 24,500,000 people. As with the first and second Estates, it too was stratified. About 500,000 individuals (two percent) were members of a professional class known as the *bourgeoisie.* These were mostly educated people who lived in France's towns and cities. The wealthiest members of the bourgeoisie formed an upper class known as the *haute bourgeoisie.* Below them were the middling sorts who formed the *petit bourgeoisie.* Below them was a meaner sort that would later be known as the *proletariat.* Beneath this bottom tier were peasants who lived in the countryside and worked the land.

Each of the three orders had problems. The French Monarch was on the verge of bankruptcy and having difficulties raising the money he needed to operate his government and household. As the Age of Reason wore on, the clerical upper crust had become secular, and the French people had become resentful of the authority it wielded and the abusive way in which it wielded its authority. Wealthy members of the haute bourgeoisie were heavily taxed. Because the best places in government and in commerce were reserved for aristocrats, educated members of the petit bourgeoisie had little opportunity to advance or to improve their lives.

The French economy was being strangled by regulation. The

bureaucrats of France's over-managed, highly centralized government had developed a steadily expanding network of rules and procedures to channel money into the King's coffers. A side effect of over-regulation was corruption, which permeated French society. With commerce thwarted and movement of food products obstructed at every intersection, financial calamities were frequent and starvation was a constant threat, especially for France's peasants whose lives depended on the success of each year's harvest.

Seeds of reform had been sown by two men of whom Jefferson knew little or nothing. Voltaire was a well-born commoner who became rich, famous, and celebrated by satirizing France's all-powerful Catholic Church and the corruptions of the French monarchy. Jean-Jacques Rousseau began his life as a poor member of France's underclass. Through his writings, he elevated himself to become a member of Diderot's celebrated society of encyclopedists. He gained notoriety by writing critiques condemning the inequality of the feudal system that tied France's peasants to the land and deprived them of political rights.

Voltaire and Rousseau were clarions for reform but they were not reformers, which is to say they did not implement new policies or organize movements to force changes in policy. They reshaped the French Mind with their trenchant words.

Anne Robert Jacques Turgot was a reformer. After training at the Sorbonne to take Holy Orders, he entered public service. He held administrative positions in Paris until 1761 when he was appointed

Intendant of the impoverished district of Limousin. He labored there for thirteen years. In 1774, the new King called him back to Paris to serve as his Comptroller General. In this position, Turgot directed the finances of the government.

Turgot pursued his work in the light of his novel view of man in society. By solving the problems he faced as a member of society, he would help society advance toward a state of ultimate perfection. When Jefferson arrived in Paris, virtually all the people he met shared Turgot's view. Not only did they believe that history is progressive, they were anxious to apply their knowledge to hasten its advance.

The author of the *Declaration of Independence* never encountered this idea in America. During his college years, which began in 1760 and ended in 1762, he had been mentored by his colony's brightest men. Scholarly Scottish cleric William Small introduced him to the Classics and Moral Philosophy. He became a dissenter and a skeptic while listening to Governor Francis Fauquier condemn the orthodoxy of the Anglican Church and commend the natural religion of heretical Lord Bolingbroke. He subsequently became expert in the Common Law under the guidance of the virtuous George Wythe.

The French and Indian War was winding down when Jefferson completed his college education and began his legal training. The year after the treaty of peace was signed, Parliament implemented a plan to raise revenues in the colonies to help fund their defense. The outrage Parliament's plan triggered shook the colonies and ignited resistance that quickly blossomed into a national political movement. Jefferson watched it being born while reading the law with George Wythe.

The best and brightest men in Jefferson's generation were not doing what their counterparts were doing in France. As France's cognoscenti pondered how to solve the problems of man in society, patriots in America were building a network of insurgents to obstruct the objectionable policies of the British Parliament. In 1773, as the illuminati of Paris communed in exclusive salons, Jefferson joined the patriotic movement and began applying his lawyer skills to throw off the yoke of British rule.

It is hardly surprising that Jefferson did not invoke the French concept of Progress in his draft of the *Declaration of Independence.* The men who orchestrated the American Revolutionary were engaged in a power struggle arguably unprecedented in the annals of human history. Their objective was to seize the governmental authority exercised by the English Parliament and exercise it themselves in their local legislatures. Jefferson echoed his compatriots by invoking the philosophical abstractions they invoked to rationalize their *coup d'état.* If he spent time debating enlightened French ideas with his patriotic peers, he did not mention it. If he explored them privately, he left no record showing what he learned.

Given the momentum of the patriotic movement and the calamities of the war, Jefferson must have been astonished by the passivity of France's cognoscenti. These world-wise cosmopolitans, cloistered in private conclaves, seemed content to ponder and deliberate.

Curbing the abusive power of the Catholic Church was a matter to debate but not to settle with law or political pressure. The same for France's backward economy and bankrupt monarchy. Jefferson was particularly disturbed by the inequality and injustice inherent in France's hereditary society. With a few notable exceptions, such as Lafayette, the illuminati of the Parisian salons were content to condemn these problems and continue with their privileged lives. Why? I suspect for the best among them, although they were progressives, they understood that the ignorant masses could not govern themselves.

Jefferson approached this matter as an architect-engineer, not as a theorist. Sitting quietly and contemplating the Hôtel de Salm was a Jeffersonian trait. Sitting quietly and contemplating Turgot's concept of Progress was not. Nor was he given to speculating on nature of the common good or what would happen if the illiterate masses were given political rights.

When Jefferson arrived in Paris, he was willing to overlook these conflicts. He was willing to do this because he had come to France to re-make himself in the image of men like the marquis de Chastellux. Chastellux may have been better than the rest of the men in his social class, but as a whole they measured each other by their speculative skills. Jefferson soon came to understand this because he was on the lookout for it. (A year after he arrived, Jefferson explained to his friend Charles Bellini that he had come to France to "examine the condition of the great" and "to appreciate the value of their circumstances".)

To become a man of standing in the marquis' circle, Jefferson had to develop speculative skills. He also had to adopt the worldview that shaped the marquis' thoughts and guided his actions. He spent his first year in France mastering these tricky skills. With help from Cabanis, he internalized the concept of Progress and became a progressive. Trying his hand at theorizing, he invented a new twist to the well-traveled idea that "the earth belongs to the living." (Jefferson attached to it the provision that a new society forms every 19 years.)

As a progressive, he accepted that it was his duty to help reform France. He did this as a member of the duc de la Rochefoucauld's circle and as an advisor to Lafayette when Lafayette assumed a leadership role in the National Assembly. When Jefferson returned home in 1789, he continued in his role as a progressive reformer by joining his friend's opposition party and waging a "second American Revolution." His victory in the presidential election of 1800 put America back on the path of progress. As his country's third President, Jefferson dedicated himself to making the United States the protector of the new world order.

chapter nine

Activating the Plan

Jefferson and his daughter Martha (whom he called "Patsy") reached Cowes on the Isle of Wight on 25 July 1784. They remained there several days while Patsy recovered from the strain of the ocean voyage. On 31 July they landed at Le Harve. Three days later, they started on the final leg of their journey in a coach bound for Paris.

Harve lay at the mouth of the River Seine 120 miles northwest of the French capital. The road followed the course of the River. During their journey, Jefferson, his daughter, and the panther skin Jefferson purchased in Philadelphia, passed through miles of prosperous Norman farmland. Jefferson described it saying that "no soil could be more fertile, better cultivated, or more elegantly improved."

About three quarters of the way to Paris, the road passed through the castle of the duc de la Rochefoucauld. Jefferson's coach would have stopped there to pay a toll. Jefferson would visit the castle again fourteen months later, this time to be welcomed into the duc's close-knit circle of reformers.

When Jefferson was not making mental notes about French agriculture, he was probably pondering how to implement his plan. This probably led the savage from the American mountains to think about the four men he knew in France and how they might assist him in accomplishing his private objective.

First on Jefferson's list was the marquis de Chastellux. Jefferson had hosted the marquis during a weeklong visit to Monticello in the spring of 1782. In Jefferson's mind, the marquis was the ideal man—poised, knowledgeable, and charming. Jefferson's second acquaintance was his Charlottesville neighbor, Philippe Mazzei. Jefferson knew the Italian nobleman to be a world traveler and admired him as an authority on the production of wine. Jefferson's third acquaintance was the marquis de Lafayette. During his second term as Governor of Virginia, Jefferson had corresponded with General Washington's trusted lieutenant. Jefferson knew him to be "a friend of Liberty" and as one of the wealthiest men in France. Jefferson's fourth connection was his former colleague in the Continental Congress. Benjamin Franklin was now His Excellency, America's Ambassador to France. At this early moment in his tour, it seems unlikely that Jefferson would have understood that his former colleague was adored by virtually every literate person in France.

For the proud, secretive Virginian, Chastellux posed a tricky problem. To insinuate himself upon the discriminating member of the Royal Academy might lower the marquis' estimation of his recent American acquaintance. The same for Lafayette. How could Jefferson establish himself as the peer of such an eminent man while dunning him for favors? Anyway, Lafayette was not in France. He would not arrive from America until January 1785.

Mazzei was a different story. Jefferson had given him valuable assistance. He had arranged for him to take a home near to Jefferson's own in Charlottesville. He had helped him start a vineyard, and he endorsed his venture as an arms dealer during the American Revolution. Unfortunately, the Italian gadfly did not count for much among France's cognoscenti. And like Lafayette, he was not in France. Mazzei would not reach Paris until the summer of 1785.

Having paid his toll, Jefferson's coachman drove on to Montes-la-Jolie where the coach ferried across the Seine. South of the river was more farmland. Gradually it became hilly and wooded. By and by the coach came to another town, Saint-Germain-en-Laye. At its center was the gardened palace where James II of England had taken refuge during Parliament's Glorious Revolution against him in 1688. The coach turned there and followed along the bend in the river. Jefferson heard its noisy clanking before he saw *le Machine de Marly* whose fourteen pumps made it the largest mechanical device in the known world.

Turning from the river, the coach ascended the hill that overlooked the noisy contraption. As it climbed the wooded slope, Jefferson caught a glimpse of an elegant chateau on its crest. This was the storied residence of Madame du Barry, Louis XV's last mistress. The coach continued on to the village of Marly-le Roi where it passed a once-grand palace of Louis XIV. Jefferson would return to this neglected park two years later with Maria Cosway.

They were on the road to Versailles, the home of the French King and the seat of his government. A short way along this road, the coach turned to the east. Jefferson was now in the final phase of his long trip. To his left, in the distance, was Mount Valerian whose boardinghouse Jefferson would later patronize.

Passing by the resort town of St Cloud, the coach crossed the Seine again. Skirting the royal game park at la Bois de Boulogne, it came to Auteuil then to Passy where the road ran on the river's quay. Franklin lived in Passy. He had an apartment on the estate of l'Hôtel de Valentinois. This splendid estate was one of several that overlooked the river there. Jefferson admired the meticulously manicured gardens, which he found as interesting as the architecture of the residences they garlanded.

Jefferson's thoughts turned again to his project and the role His Excellency might play in it. Jefferson had worked with Franklin in the Second Continental Congress. They had served with John Adams on the committee the Congress created to draft the document declaring that the American colonies were severing their political bands with England. But while the two men had worked together on this famous project, they had not been close.

Franklin was as much to blame as Jefferson since neither man formed close personal relationships with their congressional colleagues. Franklin engaged with them but avoided intimacy. Jefferson understood why. It was for the same reason Jefferson did. He was engaged in a larger project. As usual, Franklin was shaping himself in the minds of others. In France during the American Revolution, this had been part of a grand strategy. The American Ambassador transformed himself then into an American "homespun" and became the personification of America.

Jefferson surely understood that Franklin was integrating himself into the minds of the people. He probably understood that Franklin was shaping himself for posterity. Cementing his folklore image as "fur hat Franklin" was a central part of this business. Jefferson might have also known that his iconic superior was preparing another volume of his memoirs.

Whatever the particulars were, Jefferson knew Franklin well enough to understand that Franklin was not going to interrupt his own project to promote Jefferson's.

The costumed sage perceived Paris as a galaxy filled with solar systems. This idea formed the core of Jefferson's new connection with Franklin. Franklin orbited in countless Parisian social circles. This made him a key factor in the success of Jefferson's enterprise in France. Jefferson would consult the village sage. He would find out who printed Franklin's works and print a few dozen copies of the manuscript he was about to assemble. He would then give copies to a few chosen members of Franklin's illuminated circles. In this offhanded way, Franklin would help Jefferson complete his private mission.

chapter ten

Franklin's Social Circles

*B*enjamin Franklin reached Paris on 21 December 1776. Two days later, he met with his fellow commissioner, Silas Deane. Arthur Lee may have joined them. The commissioners drafted a memorandum for comte de Vergennes, announcing that the American Congress had empowered them to negotiate a treaty of amity and commerce and requesting an interview. The next day Franklin's teenage grandson, William Temple Franklin, drove to Versailles where he delivered the message to the Foreign Minister. Vergennes told the boy he would give him his response at 9:00 the next morning. Young Temple stayed that night at Versailles. In the morning, the minister informed him that he would meet the commissioners the following day.

At this meeting, Vergennes told the Americans to "lie low". He told Franklin to conduct himself as a private citizen who had come to France on family business. When he came to Versailles, he was to do so incognito. Before excusing himself, Vergennes informed his guest that French ports would be open to American vessels.

Franklin returned to Paris, settled into more comfortable quarters at Hôtel de Hambourg on rue Jacob, and commenced his wait for the diplomatic ice to melt. In the meantime, he went on with his "family" business. The most pressing part of it was arranging loans.

The most time-consuming was fending off callers who wanted to fight for the cause in America.

Lying low did not prevent Franklin from attending a salon event hosted by Madame du Deffand, evidently in the last week of 1776. Following Vergennes's instructions, Franklin attended in the guise of a private citizen. In a letter to Horace Walpole, the marquise noted that he wore "a fur cap on his head and glasses on his nose" and was surrounded by "important partisans of his cause."

On the 18 January 1777, Franklin received his first dinner invitation. It was from the duchess d'Anville who requested he come the following week to "our home". Franklin, in other words, knew where she lived. This is not surprising. Franklin was a friend of long-standing to several physiocratic economists who were members of her circle. It is quite possible that he met the duchesse and her son Louis-Alexandre, duc de la Rochefoucauld, during his 1767 and 1769 vacations to Paris.

A package he received from the duc three days before the dinner suggests that they had conferred during the previous weeks. On 20 January, the duc sent Franklin "50. Exemplars of the American Confederation translated", which "will be publicated [sic] in the Journal *Des Affaires de l'Amérique*." His note confirms that the duc had begun his great project of translating key American political documents into French. Franklin, it seems, had already begun to serve as his reference and editorial assistant. Participation in this enterprise may explain why on 8 January Franklin moved his residence to Hôtel de Hambourg: it was across the street from the Hôtel le

Rochefoucauld, which made interacting with the duc most convenient. Franklin remained at the Hôtel de Hambourg until Chaumont offered him an apartment on his estate in Passy.

Duchess d'Anville was said to be the most brilliant woman in Paris and "the friend of economists". Abigail Adams described her as tall, lean and surrounded by academicians. She followed the *noblesse oblige* of her ancient family by striving to improve the life of the peasants who tended her estates. There is every indication that her interests extended to improving that state of agriculture throughout France. The salon she hosted focused on progress through economic reform and agricultural modernization.

During his earlier trips to Paris, Franklin had met Mirabeau and du Pont. He may also have met Quesnay. Turgot, however, was not in Paris in those moments so Franklin probably did not meet him. While in London, he might have encountered Louis–Alexandre and his English friend, agricultural reformer Arthur Young. Quesnay died in 1774, but the others formed the core for the duchesse's circle. The marquis de Condorcet was another important member. In August of 1777, he became the permanent secretary of the Royal Academy of Sciences, of which Franklin had been a member since 1772. Others notable members of the Academy were Buffon, Daubenton, Lavoisier, and Malesherbes. Some of these men probably joined gatherings that Franklin attended at l'Hôtel le Rochefoucauld.

Louis-Alexandre's interests in agriculture extended back at least to the early 1760s when he and his cousin François toured England with Arthur Young. Returned to France, the duc's interest in improving French agriculture lured him to the salon of the marquis de Mirabeau, which began about the time of Franklin's first visit to Paris. The marquis attracted his guest by serving them supper before reading a paper. A disciple of François Quesnay, these papers treated aspects of *physiocratic* economics. Quesnay sometimes attended these events.

Quesnay was Louis XV's physician. The king sought his advice on many matters. After his health, foremost among them were his financial difficulties. Quesnay famously crystalized them as: poor peasant, poor kingdom; poor kingdom, poor king! Quesnay's theory of economics focused on how wealth was created and distributed. His chief interest was to help the king solve his poor peasant-poor king problem. Du Pont de Nemours assisted him in this enterprise. When Turgot became Comptroller General, he made du Pont his personal secretary, and together they tried to implement reforms based on Quesnay's physiocratic principles.

Franklin had opinions about taxation economics, but in 1777 his business was building support for the American cause. Louis-Alexandre helped him do this.

Commissioner Franklin moved his residence to l'hôtel de Valentinois in early March 1777. His neighbor in nearby Auteuil was Anne-Catherine de Ligniville Helvétius. More than a year elapsed, however, before he met her. Turgot has been credited with making the introduction, which he seems to have done shortly after the time he introduced his Franklin to Pierre Cabanis. Franklin penned his first letter to the charming lady in October 1778. "I see" he said, speaking in familiar terms, "that statesmen, philosophers, historians, poets, and men of learning of all sorts, are drawn around you, and seem as willing to attach themselves to you as straws about a fine piece of amber." Not until September of the following year did she write to him. "I hoped, she sighed, "that after having told me such pretty things on paper, you would come and tell me in person . . . for I confess that I love pretty things, especially those that come to me from you."

Madame Helvétius's husband had died in 1771. The next year she purchased the Auteuil estate of artist Quentin La Tour, who was in the process of a mental breakdown and about to return to Saint-Quentin in the north of France. Her situation in Auteuil, where she entertained a menagerie of animals and guests in three acres of gardens, was probably beyond her childhood dreams.

Anne-Catherine's father was a member of an old, impoverished family from the Lorraine district in the upper eastern corner of France. Her mother was a well-placed commoner. As one of twenty children in a family without wealth, Anne-Catherine's prospects had not been bright. At some point during her girlhood, she moved to a convent. She might have spent the rest of her life there had her mother's sister not invited her to come to Paris. Madame Françoise d'Issembourg d'Happoncourt de Graffigny was an aspiring author. She called her niece to join her in 1746 as her career was about to bloom. The following year she published her first novel. The success of *Letters from a Peruvian Woman* made her a minor celebrity among the literati of Paris, and her home on rue Saint-Hyacinthe (a block from Saint Roch Church on rue Saint-Honoré) became a popular meeting place for Parisian littérateurs.

While helping her aunt manage her events, Anne-Catherine mingled with the brightest lumieres of the Parisian galaxy. Montesquieu, Saint-Lambert, Diderot, Fontenelle, Rousseau, and Voltaire were among her admirers. Turgot appeared in 1749. The following year, he is reputed to have proposed marriage to Madame's beautiful niece. Perhaps it was his lack of assets that caused her to decline.

A year later, wealthy farmer general Claude Helvétius offered the young lady his hand, and Anne-Catherine accepted. Over the next twenty years, the mistress of Voré au Perche provided companionship and managed the social affairs of her charming husband. During the first years of their happy marriage, she helped him complete his famous transition from tax collector to *philosophe*. Madame did this by enticing guests from her aunt's salon to Voré. Claude would pick their brains between lavish meals and garden events and then integrate the information he gathered into his new rationalistic Science of Man. Although *de l'Esprit* was universally condemned, it was one of the most widely read and consequential books of the French Enlightenment. What Madame thought of it is not known.

Claude Helvétius was a regular guest at the dinner parties of Baron d'Holbach. At these gatherings he mingled with Diderot, Grimm,

Raynal, Morellet, Chastellux, Saint-Lambert, and other eminent cosmopolitans of Paris. The roots of his social science are in the baron's philosophy. Holbach was a vehement materialist whose intellectual reputation traces to the Lockean proposition that all mental activity derives from sensation. He supplemented this idea with the Cartesian vision of matter as extension and motion to create an atheistic mélange, which condemned Christianity, monarchical government, and hereditary privilege as obstacles to the good of society and individual happiness. Having become a Freemason in 1747, Helvétius interpreted the baron's sweeping critique in terms of the social virtue he practiced in his fellowcraft: benevolence, charity, morality, truth, justice, education.

Helvétius was inspired by his faith in the idea that promulgating these virtues would improve conditions in his society. He sought to actualize his ideal by creating a masonic lodge in which learned men of similar good will could learn and disseminate them. To honor her husband's memory, Madame Helvétius helped his brother in the Craft, astronomer Jerome Lalande, create a "learned Masonic society". Shortly before Franklin reached France, the Lodge of the Nine Sisters received its charter. In 1778, Franklin joined the lodge. Later that year, he was elected its "Venerated Master".

Madame also established a salon in her Auteuil home. It became a gathering place for scholarly Masons and old cosmopolitans who shared her husband's interests in science and progress. After leaving his post in the royal government, Turgot began to attend. His influence, together with its Masonic drapery attracted several bright young lights, most of who were (or became) Freemasons. In addition to Cabanis, and Volney, these included Tracy, Pinel, Chamfort, and Roederer. Years later, Jefferson became acquainted with Madame and befriended some of the young men in her entourage, but there is no indication that he became a regular participant in her salon.

Elisabeth Françoise Sophie Lalive de Bellegarde was the daughter of Farmer General Louis Denis Lalive de Bellegarde and Josèphe Prouveur. In keeping with the times, she was married at the age of eighteen (in 1748) to a young man she hardly knew. Her cousin, with whom she had lived through her teenage years, described Claude Constant César, Comte d' Houdetot as "a young man of quality, but without fortune: aged twenty-two, a gambler, ugly as the devil, and little advanced in the service." This was not entirely correct since his father, as another account observed, authored a marriage agreement in which the marquis d'Houdetot dowered his son with "18,000 livres a year in farms in Normandy, and the guidon of gendaremerie which he had bought for him." [See: *The Nation*. Vol. 72. June 1901. 451.] Count d'Houdetot was a military officer who rose in rank through the Seven Years War. In service during these impressionable years, he left his young wife in the company of her cousin, Madame d'Epinay. Madame d'Epinay's relationship with Baron Grimm brought her cousin into contact with Diderot, members of his entourage, her life-long lover (Saint-Lambert), and Jean-Jacques Rousseau.

Madame d'Epinay described her as having "a continual air of idleness, especially when her lover is away, to let everything drift, and to forget constantly where she is and what she needs to do." Rousseau was charmed by her. Having encountered her in a chance meeting at his cottage on Madame d'Epinay's estate, he fell madly in love with her. "Like the ivy that takes the form of the tree to which it clings," he later remembered, "her opinions, tastes, and inclinations all received the imprint of the person she loved." [See: Leo Damrosch. *Jean Jacques Rousseau – Restless Genius.* Houghton Mifflin. 2005. 270.]

Sophie d'Houdetot did not return Rousseau's love, but his equalitarian views on society became the theme of her salon. When she opened it is not clear, but it was probably after she settled in Sannois, which she seems to have done prior to the American Revolution. She and her friends took a dutiful interest in the war, celebrating Liberty as an essential part of the march of human progress. Her reputation as "a collector" of Americans seems to rest on the friendship she developed with Michel Guillaume Jean de Crèvecœur which began a few months after the famous "fête champêtre" she hosted for Franklin in the summer of 1781.

Crèvecœur was said to be the son of "an old Norman friend" of Madame's. He returned to France in the fall of 1781 after nearly thirty years in America. Welcoming him into her salon, Madame presented him to key members of her circle, including the duc de la Rochefoucauld and his cousin Liancourt, d'Alembert, La Harpe, Grimm, and Franklin. France's cognoscenti perceived Crèvecœur as a valuable source of information about America. His *Letters from an*

American Farmer (1782) helped shape the French image of America as a wilderness utopia. His maps were said to fascinate Louis XVI, who was among other things an amateur cartographer.

Where Madame Helvétius's guests expected to discuss matters relating to social and natural science, Sophie d'Houdetot's guests expected to discuss Politics. She invited Jefferson to one of her events in the spring of 1785. By his time, Franklin had retired from the cocktail circuit and was not an active participant in her circle. In Madame d'Houdetot's circle, Jefferson would have encountered young reformers and future revolutionaries rather than the Masons, scientists, and philosophes who enlightened Madame Helvetius's salon.

chapter eleven

Jefferson's First Nine Months in Paris

On 6 August 1784, Jefferson, his daughter, and his panther skin, passed by Franklin's residence in Passy on the final leg of their journey to Paris. A short way on, their coach turned onto the grandest avenue they had ever seen, the beautiful Champs Elysees. Jefferson had finally reached Paris! To mark the occasion, he may have addressed his daughter. He may have noted the greatness of the city and the greatness of the men it produced. He may have instructed "Patsy" to make the most of the opportunities awaiting her there. No doubt she promised to do so.

The Jeffersons' destination was l'Hôtel d'Orléans on rue Richelieu at le Palais Royal. Le Palais Royal was the home of the King's distant cousin. Paris had for some time been experiencing rapid growth. The duc d'Orleans sought to capitalize on it by transforming his palatial residence into the world's first shopping mall and emporium. Construction had not yet been completed when the Jeffersons arrived at their hotel.

The emporium next door had already become a popular gathering place. Shoppers filled its arcades. Pleasure-seekers filled the brothels in the apartments above. As these entertainments were being pursued, petit bourgeoisie malcontents in the facility's numerous coffee houses, cafés, and political clubs were debating how to overthrow France's oppressive monarchy. Like Franklin, Lafayette, and perhaps Mazzei, the duc d'Orleans was a Freemason. More than that, he was Grand Master for half the lodges in France! Large numbers of the new men who gathered in the political societies that met in his bustling palace were members of lodges that the duc supervised. These men started the uprising that blossomed into the French Revolution. It began in the garden of the Café de Foye in the northwest corner of the duc's emporium.

After settling himself, Jefferson, perhaps accompanied by Patsy, drove to Passy and called on Franklin. Having learned that Franklin's printer was Philippe-Denis Pierres, Jefferson paid the printer a visit during which he seems to have made arrangements to print the manuscript he would spend the next eight months preparing.

Jefferson was a detail-oriented engineer. He therefore seems out of character in the vague way he treated his affairs during these months. It seems that he was not well. He was also mastering his duties as a member of Franklin's staff. But I suspect the real reason for his silence was that he did not care for people to know how much time he was spending developing a printable manuscript. Had people understood what the Wizard of Monticello was doing beyond his veil, they might have wondered what his purpose was in creating the text.

Put yourself in Jefferson's place. Imagine that you are a fiercely proud and private person, that you have just arrived in a foreign country where you are unfamiliar with how things are done and where you barely understand the language. If you make a false step, you might draw attention to yourself. You might even embarrass yourself in the eyes of people you want to impress! Best to remain out of sight.

Jefferson may have thought he could do this at the Hôtel d'Orleans on rue Richelieu. But something was evidently wrong there. Shortly after Jefferson visited Franklin, he and Patsy relocated to a hotel by the same name on the other side of the River Seine.

Their new lodgings were near the grand residences of the marquis de Lafayette, the duchesse d'Anville, the marquis de Condorcet, and the shop of the man who would print Jefferson's book. During the two months Jefferson and his daughter resided there, Jefferson seems to have restricted his socializing to official functions. Abigail Adams shed some light on this. John Adams had accompanied her from London to Paris shortly after Jefferson arrived in Paris.

In letters Abigail wrote to her niece and her sister on 5 September, she boasted that she had "dined abroad many times." She did not mention Jefferson, but he was probably present at some of these dinners such as the one hosted by American Consul Thomas Barclay and his wife Mary.

It seems Jefferson was not present during Abigail's famous visit to the Auteuil home of Madame Helvétius later that August. What I find most interesting in Abigail's account of this affair is the haphazard way Franklin introduced of his colleague's wife to this dear friend. I expect Franklin operated with the same inattentiveness where Jefferson was concerned.

Because Jefferson was familiar with Franklin's manners, I doubt that he was surprised. He went to France with the understanding that he would replace Franklin when the old man finally decided to return home. In accordance with this unspecific plan, Jefferson was prepared to lie low until that moment came. In the meantime, he would finish his book. He would then have a conversation piece he could give selected people in Franklin's circles.

Jefferson left nothing to suggest that he met Madame Helvétius or the bright young men in her entourage in the last months of 1784 or the first months of 1785. This makes the letter he wrote Abigail Adams on 21 June 1785 noteworthy. In it, Jefferson announced that he had visited Madame d'Houdetot. Said Jefferson:

> *I took a trip yesterday to Sannois and commenced an acquaintance with the old Countess Houdetot. I received much pleasure from it and hope it has opened a door of admission for me to the circle of literati with which she is environed.*

These vapor trails suggest to me that Jefferson did not appear in the salons of Paris until after he received his books from the printer, which he did on 10 May 1785. Prior to this, he seemed satisfied accoutering himself for his future post. He chaperoned his 12-year-old daughter, purchased wardrobes and other paraphernalia for himself and Patsy, and he hunted for a permanent residence.

After attiring himself in clothing that was suitable for Parisian society, Jefferson focused on mastering the duties he would have as America's second Ambassador to France. He conferred periodically with Franklin and Adams. He attended weekly Court functions. He drafted official documents, and managed the correspondence of the embassy.

Jefferson also tended to his health, which was below par during his "seasoning" period. One supposes that his home cures included self-guided walking tours through the city and visiting bookstores, many of which were in the vicinity of his second residence on rue des Petits-Augustins, which ran behind the Hôtel des Monnaies where the marquis de Condorcet resided.

Two months after reaching Paris, Jefferson's situation changed. On October 17th, he signed a nine-year lease for an unfurnished hôtel on cul-de-sac Taitbout. Jefferson spent a fortune furnishing his new residence. Once he had done so, he hosted his first dinner, apparently for members of his diplomatic circle.

Lafayette sent Jefferson a letter at this time advising him that his young wife, Adrienne, would be delighted to help Patsy get settled. This led a few months later to Patsy's enrollment in an exclusive girl's school, where she became a boarder.

A few weeks after moving into the Hôtel Landron, Jefferson's kinsman (through his wife's family) arrived in Paris and joined his household. Prior to departing for France, in a strange coded correspondence, Jefferson had assured William Short that he would employ the hopeful young attorney if the Congress authorized him to have a secretary. In private discussions, Jefferson probably acquainted his kinsman with his book project.

I believe Jefferson delayed work on his manuscript until he had established his residence at Hôtel Landron. There he had a suitably private place to work. When his kinsman arrived in mid-November, he gained an assistant to help him organize the jumble of information in his binders. With significant help from Short, Jefferson then began to assemble and fine-tune the advertisement he would use to establish himself in the eyes of best and brightest people in Paris.

Given the importance of the project, it is not surprising that in his *Autobiography,* which he wrote in 1821, Jefferson pictured his life during these months in terms of printing his book. Said Jefferson:

These memoranda were on loose papers, bundled up without order, and filled with duplication. I thought this a good occasion to embody their substance, which I did in the order of M. Marbois' queries, so as to answer his wish and to arrange them for my own use.

Some friends with whom I occasionally communicated wished for copies; but there being too many to transcribe by hand, I proposed to get a few printed for their gratification . . . On my arrival at Paris I found this could be done for a fourth of what it cost in Philadelphia. I therefore corrected and enlarged them, and had 200 copies printed, under the title of Notes on Virginia.

Thomas Jefferson may not have been like the rest of us, but he was still just a man. He had a variety of quirks and peculiar behavioral tendencies. There is no doubt that he followed these natural tendencies in compiling the bundles of loose pages he brought with him from America into a printable manuscript. Conspicuous among the quirks he followed while creating the manuscript for his *Notes on Virginia* was the way he did it beyond his Wizard-of-Oz veil.

chapter twelve

Notes on Virginia

Thomas Jefferson expended considerable effort transforming the notes he brought with him from America into a printable manuscript. In the letter he wrote to James Madison on 11 May 1785, Jefferson informed Madison that his printer had finished printing his book the previous day. That it took Jefferson nine months to complete the project is further evidence that he created his manuscript *after* he arrived in France.

The history of the book began in early February of 1781, when Jefferson received a list of questions from the French consul in Philadelphia. After leaving his post as Governor of Virginia on June 1st of that year, answering these questions seems to have become the center of the retired patriot's activities. Jefferson sent Monsieur Marbois his responses on 20 December 1781. (The fact that this was four months before Jefferson met the marquis de Chastellux is significant.) Sending Marbois his answers to did not end the business for Jefferson. He continued gathering information up to the time of his departure for France in June of 1784.

As noted above, Jefferson remembered in his *Autobiography* that when he arrived in France, "these memoranda were on loose papers, bundled up without order, and filled with duplication." In other words, his collection of data had grown far beyond the communiqué he sent to Marbois thirty months before. Turning this disorganized bundle of papers into a printable manuscript was not a trivial task. That it took nine months is not surprising. It would have probably taken far longer had William Short not been there to lend a hand.

Before he could begin the deskwork, Jefferson needed to acquire a few key reference texts. First among these was Buffon's 12-volume *Histoire Naturelle.* (Jefferson referred to specific pages and passages of this work in his text.) [See: Massachusetts Historical Society. Thomas Jefferson Papers. 1789 Catalog of Books. Page 21.]

I expect that Jefferson waited until after he had his reference library in place before he began the work of organizing the jumble of information into the first draft of his book. Such a draft would have been what he and his assistant worked from to produce the printer's copy.

Amazingly, the Massachusetts Historical Society appears to have this document. Ann Bentley, Curator at the Society, has noted that authors did not typically get their manuscripts back from their printers. This is a significant point. Anyone who examines the Massachusetts Historical Society's document will see immediately that a printer, especially one who was not fluent in English (Jefferson's was not) could not have created a book from these barely legible sheets.

How did Jefferson overcome this problem? William Short could read Jefferson's handwriting, and he could consult the author minute-to-minute to clarify the meanings of the crossed out lines and interwoven insertions that filled the draft Jefferson was conscientiously reworking. I expect that as Jefferson scratched and pasted his corrections into the manuscript now in the possession of the Massachusetts Historical Society, Short transcribed the corrections into a clean copy for the printer. The printer worked from Short's clean copy, not from the dog-eared draft Jefferson retained and passed down through his granddaughter to posterity.

Jefferson learned from Chastellux in the spring of 1782 that France's cognoscenti were more interested in some things than in others. When you read his book, you will find that Jefferson devoted a disproportionate amount of time expounding on these topics. France's best and brightest men and women perceived America as an enlightened social experiment and were anxious to know that it was producing the results their theory of social progress predicted.

This hopeful theory was a rational system that rested on religious-like faith in the generative power of Nature and a corresponding confidence that progress follows when Nature's order is unfettered. In this context, democracy, social equality, and laissez faire economics, were all, in theory, instruments of progress.

As noted above, this was not an optic Jefferson had encountered in America. Because Jefferson had not mastered it when he produced his book, the analyses it contained were slightly out of tune to the French ear. Some subjects Jefferson addressed were more interesting to France's progressives than others. Because Jefferson understood this, I believe he expanded his comments on those subjects. He shaped them, however, to promote his private purpose, not simply to convey information.

I believe the idea of raising himself on the strength of his book crystalized in Jefferson's mind after he accepted Congress's 1784 invitation to join Franklin and Adams in France. The centerpiece of this endeavor—refuting the theory of comte de Buffon—seems to have crystalized in Jefferson's mind on his way to visit Charles Thomson in Philadelphia in April of 1784. If it occurred to him before that time, it seems he would have purchased the "uncommonly large panther skin" he later delivered to Buffon in a market more convenient to him than one in the City of Brotherly Love.

During his first months in Paris, Jefferson participated in enough conversations with Franklin, Adams, Barclay and other members of the diplomatic corps to gauge the intellectual environment. I believe he measured himself in this light and concluded that the things he had to say would be sufficiently interesting to the Parisian cognoscenti that he could promote himself by challenging Buffon.

Unfortunately, working in isolation in his library at Hôtel Landron, Jefferson got carried away. In the process of advertising himself as a scientist, which he did in Chapter 6 of his book, he manufactured an attack on the comte that verged on insolence. While advertising himself as a expert on constitutional government in Virginia, which he in did Chapter 13 of his book, Jefferson launched an attack on the Virginia legislature and Virginia's new constitution that he would later regret. While advertising himself as an author of the progressive Report of the Revisors, which he did in Chapter 14 of his book, Jefferson unleashed an embarrassingly unscientific diatribe against the Negro Race.

Perhaps his most successful advertisement was his account of the plan of the Revisors for a system of public education, also found in Chapter 14, which Jefferson himself conceived and authored. He neglected to mention that Virginia's legislature had rejected his idea.

Jefferson received 200 printed copies of his book on 10 May 1785. He reported in his Autobiography that "I gave a very few copies to some particular persons in Europe, and sent the rest to my friends in America." Jefferson identified the people he favored, but he did so in a haphazard fashion. This owes to the fact that it took him more than two years to complete the business, and long before he did it ceased to interest him. Several recipients are mentioned in letters he wrote. The first to receive copies were Chastellux, Buffon via Chastellux, Daubenton via Chastellux, Adams, Franklin, Lafayette, abbe Morellet, Madison via M. Doradour, Richard Price via Adams, Wythe via Mr. Joddrel, G. K. Van Hagendorp, Mr. Otto, Monroe via Mr. Otto, Charles Thomson via Franklin's grandnephew, Jonathan Williams (and thus perhaps Williams himself), shady Mr. Williamos, William Carmichael, Thomas Barclay, and John Page.

Others who received copies included William Short, who probably drafted the copy Jefferson sent to the printer; Philippe Mazzei introduced him to a number of Italian naturalists several of whom also received copies; Philadelphians David Rittenhouse, Francis Hopkinson, and Benjamin Barton contributed material to the project; Colonel David Humphrey was the secretary of the American delegation in Paris; François Barbé-Marbois circulated the original questionnaire. General Washington was the Father of his country. Maria Cosway was the charming courtesan Jefferson briefly courted in the fall of 1786. I did not check whether all of the 145 copies Coolie Verner said Jefferson sent in crates to Madison, Wythe, and Alexander Donald were firsts editions, but if they were, Jefferson distributed more than 200 copies.

There is no record that Jefferson gave copies of his book to the duc de la Rochefoucauld, the marquis de Condorcet, or du Pont de Nemours. Nor is there a record showing that Volney, Tracy, or Cabanis, Madame Helvétius, Madame d'Houdetot, or duchesse d'Anville, Madame Necker, Madame de Stael, Madame de Tott, or comtesse de Tessé were recipients. The French National Library received a copy, but there is no record showing that Jefferson sent one to the French King or to any of the new men who helped to overthrow him.

A few weeks after Jefferson started distributing his book, Franklin returned home. Jefferson replaced him on 7 July 1785. The usefulness of his book as an advertisement faded after his elevation. It must have dawned on Jefferson about this time that to approach Franklin in the estimation of France's best men and women, he needed to know about more than the state of affairs in Virginia. He needed to be conversant in things that affected their lives. Fine-tuning his understanding of affairs in France and the French people therefore became a primary focus after Jefferson finished his book.

chapter thirteen

Pierre Jean Georges Cabanis

$\mathcal{T}$he man who became the Sage of Monticello was brilliant and read a lot, but to become enlightened he needed instruction from someone who was versed in the French concept of Progress and understood how it knitted into the worldview of France's cognoscenti. During Jefferson's time there, only two men could have explained these things to Jefferson. One was the marquis de Condorcet. The other was the marquis' future brother-in-law, Pierre Cabanis.

Both these men had unique insights into Turgot's signature theory, and both had sufficient standing in the opinion of the reserved Virginian to instruct him. Only Cabanis, however, was on sufficiently intimate terms with the aspiring American and willing to conduct him through a program of instruction.

Condorcet was the most brilliant man of his age. He was widely recognized as the greatest living *philosophe.* His accomplishments spread across the natural and applied sciences, through the new social sciences and into politics and literature. He became the permanent secretary of the Royal Academy of Sciences in 1773 and held the post until the royal academies were abolished in 1793. In 1782 he was elected one of the forty members of the French Academy.

Cabanis had not become a member of the Royal Academy of Sciences when it was abolished, but he was a elected to its successor institution, the National Institute for the Arts and Sciences, that was established to replace it. When the French Academy was reestablished in 1803, Cabanis was elected to be among its forty members.

Pierre Cabanis was born in 1757 in the town of Cosnac in the province of Limousin. His father was a lawyer whose marriage brought him a castle and lands along with a wife. After his marriage, Jean Baptiste Cabanis added sheep raising and farming to his duties as chief magistrate of the lower district of Limousin. In all these capacities, he found a helpful friend in the Intendant of Limoges, Anne-Robert-Jacques Turgot. Monsieur Cabanis is remembered today as a physiocrat for his efforts in modernizing agriculture on his own lands and in his province.

Son Jean-Pierre was a brilliant but troublesome student. When at the age of fourteen he was expelled from the Doctrinaire College at de Brive-la-Gaillarde, his father sent him to Paris. Cabanis' biographer reports that the adolescent arrived in Paris with a letter of introduction from his father's friend to Antoine Roucher. Turgot's murky connection to Roucher seems to have rested on a poem Roucher wrote in honor of Marie Antoinette's marriage to the future King Louis XVI in May of 1770. Condorcet later said that Turgot had "a passion for literature and poetry." A surviving expression of this passion, which may have influenced Cabanis, is Turgot's translation of *The Aeneid* from Greek into the form of a French rhyme.

What assistance Roucher rendered young Pierre in his pursuit of education is not clear. Apart from his poem, about the only thing known of him is the city of his birth—Montpelier, the "medicine city". Perhaps this had a bearing on the courses Cabanis took during his informal studies at the University of Paris, which began in 1771 and ended two years later.

Montpellier rivaled Paris as a center for innovation in the field of Medicine. Its medical schools were leaders in the transformation of the ancient art into a modern science. They led this enterprise by evaluating illness and treatment in terms of evolving views of the nature of Man. As the 18th century wore on, these concepts proliferated into a spectrum of conflicting theories. The Newtonians who debated these subjects in Montpellier's medical schools characterized themselves as *médecins philosophes*. A primary objective in their speculation was to replace the Aristotelian metaphysics that for two thousand years had been the foundation of their craft.

Materialism represented the empirical antithesis to the Formalism that shaped Aristotle's view of Nature. Materialism manifested itself in mid-18th century French Medicine characterization of Man as a machine and the idea that the actions and functions of the human organism were properly explained in mechanical terms. Proponents of this view were characterized as Mechanicists. Mechanicists were opposed by Sensationalists. Sensationalists accepted the existence of human minds and believed that they were populated by sensations. They argued that the connection between the body and the mind had to be understood for the science of Medicine to advance.

Sensibility was the theoretical bridge that connected the body and the mental and ethical faculties of the mind. How the body communicated sense data to the mind and how the mind processed them would become focal points in Cabanis' medical research. In the mid-1790s, this field of study became known at Ideology. Cabanis is remembered today as a pioneer in the science of thinking, which in his day encompassed the disciplines of Philosophy, Physiology, and Psychology.

Four decades before Cabanis commenced his research, French *encyclopedists* commissioned the concepts he would use in an enlightened crusade against superstition and the faith-based religions that nurtured it.

Cabanis is often described as a "medical philosopher". The books in his library help clarify what this means. It included John Locke's *Essay Concerning Human Understanding* and works by Condillac, Montesquieu, Voltaire, la Mettrie, Buffon, and Rousseau.

The concepts and theories Cabanis studied in these books were building blocks in an approach to medical treatment that was still being pioneered during Cabanis' student days. The pioneers were physicians in Montpellier, France who described themselves as "vitalists". Montpellier Vitalists were crystalizing a "holistic understanding of the physical-moral relation" that would replace the mind-body duality that had originated in the rationalist philosophy of Descartes. Illness, according to the vitalists, resulted from disharmony in a patient's animal or body "economy". In the vitalist view, health signified that the organs, which comprised the organism-patient, were functioning properly. To correct a malady, the physician had to tend to the organs that were not functioning properly and restore their normal functions. In this way, the physician restored the body economy to its natural equilibrium.

Cabanis appears to have stepped onto the path of medical philosophy during his days at the University of Paris. It was a felicitous accident, in other words, that he began to prepare himself to become a *médecin philosophe* in the school of the Montpellier Vitalists. His orientation of thought and his affiliation with like-minded thinkers allowed Cabanis to become a leader in the hospital reform movement of the revolutionary and post-revolutionary eras.

Cabanis took a number of detours on his path to fame. The first began in 1773 when sixteen-year old Pierre agreed to become the secretary of Ignacy Jacob Massalski, Prince-Bishop of Vilnius. The scope of his work is not clear, but one of his responsibilities was to give French lessons to Prince Xavier, the Bishop's nephew.

Massalski had come to Paris on two official missions. The first was to persuade the French king to help the Polish-Lithuanian Commonwealth resist the impending partition of its territory by Austria and Russia. The second was to consult French scholars on behalf of the Commonwealth's new Commission of National Education, of which Massalski was a charter member. How Massalski became aware of young Cabanis is not known. One possibility is that Turgot was acquainted with matters that concerned the Bishop and arranged the introduction.

What Cabanis expected to gain from this adventure is not clear. A fortuitous event, one that he could not have foreseen, occurred while he was in Poland, however. In the fall of 1774, he met du Pont de Nemours. Their interactions took place shortly after du Pont's arrival in Warsaw and shortly before his return to Paris, which he did around the end of the year.

Du Pont had come to Poland at the request of Massalski's kinsman, Prince Adam Czartoryski. Czartoryski had invited du Pont to become a tutor to his four year-old son. As an added inducement, du Pont was also to hold the title of "Honorary Councilor of the King and the Republic of Poland." When du Pont equivocated, the Prince offered him the additional posts of Secretary for Foreign Correspondence for the Commission for Nation Education and the directorship of its Academy. In these positions, du Pont would answer to Prince-Bishop Massalski.

Du Pont accepted the Prince's offer when he made financial arrangements so du Pont could acquire an estate in Nemours, France. Du Pont set off for Warsaw two months after the death of Louis XV at Versailles on May 10 1774. As he made his way east, Turgot was elevated from Minister of Marine to Comptroller-General of France. Soon after his arrival in Warsaw, du Pont received a letter informing him that Turgot was naming him to a post in his administration. It took three months to finalize du Pont's appointment as Inspector General of Commerce. The arrangements were finally completed in December of 1774. Du Pont left for Paris around the end of the year.

Cabanis remained in Poland a few months after du Pont's

departure then returned home himself. The timing of his resignation suggests that he knew Massalski was facing a problem. The Bishop was subsequently charged with embezzling commission funds and forced to resign in disgrace. Years later he would be lynched by an angry mob.

I believe that in a passing conversation with du Pont, Cabanis discovered that the tutor–councilor was a friend of his father's friend. I believe that du Pont also told Cabanis that he had advised the Intendant of Limousin on economic matters. As he described his interactions with Turgot in Limousin, I believe that du Pont acquainted young Cabanis with his own forward-looking view on economics and with Turgot's theory of progress. Their conversations were deepening and Cabanis was taking an increasing interest this these theoretical matters when the letter arrived advising du Pont that Turgot wanted him to become his assistant.

In Paris, Cabanis discovered that his father's friend held one of the most powerful posts in France and that he had used it to appoint Roucher collector of the salt tax in Auteuil. Some say this encouraged Cabanis to think that he could gain a similar livelihood. Whether or not this was so, for several months after returning to Paris, Cabanis traveled on Roucher's literary paths. His main occupation seems to have been translating a section of *The Iliad* for a competition sponsored by the *Académie française.* Although he failed to win the prize, his work seems to have been admired by Turgot whose friends in the *Académie* included Buffon, Chastellux,

Condillac, d'Alembert, La Harpe, Saint-Lambert, and Voltaire. Perhaps Turgot persuaded one or more of them to read his young friend's work.

The disappointment the setback caused the aspiring *littérateur* would have been compounded by Turgot's dismissal. These considerations, together with mounting pressure from his father, contributed to the twenty-year-old's decision to abandon Poetry in favor of Medicine. In 1777, Cabanis began his training under "royal physician" Jean Baptiste Léon Dubreuil.

Cabanis' medical tutor was thirty-four years old and affiliated with the Charity Hospital at Saint-Germain-en-Laye. He had trained in Montpellier under Gabriel François Venel. Venel was a Montpellier Vitalist whose circle included François Boissier de Sauvages, Théophile de Bordeu, and Paul Joseph Barthez. It seems likely therefore that Dubreuil was a proponent of the philosophical approach to Medicine that Cabanis had investigated while auditing courses at the University of Paris five years before. Cabanis thus embarked on a professional career suited to his inclinations and abilities.

Cabanis was in contact with Turgot at this time. Turgot was then a prominent figure in the illuminated society that he had entered more than two decades before.

While at the Sorbonne in 1750, Turgot had delivered his famous lecture on universal history. The second section of this paper bore the heading "On the History of the Progress of the Human Mind".

His comments on the progressive nature of History attracted the attention of Diderot who recruited him to write a refutation of the metaphysical doctrines of Bishop Berkeley for his *Encyclopedie.*

Turgot thus entered a circle that included, besides Diderot, Montesquieu, d'Alembert, Helvétius, Morellet, Galiani, Raynal, and Marmontel. These celebrated cosmopolitans communed in gatherings hosted by Madame Geoffrin, Madame de Graffigny, and Baron d'Holbach. By the early 1750s, Turgot had become a welcome guest in all of their salons. He continued to circulate in them until his relocation to Limoges in 1761. By then, he was among their leading lights.

Not long after entering the salon of Madame de Graffigny, Turgot is said to have proposed marriage to her niece. The accuracy of this claim seems questionable since at this exact moment, Mademoiselle Anne Catherine de Ligniville d'Auricourt accepted the marriage proposal of wealthy Farmer General Claude Adrian Helvétius. After her husband's death in 1771, Madame sold their country estate near Remalard (70 miles southeast of Paris) and their Parisian townhome. In 1772, she relocated to a three-acre estate in Auteuil where, in the spring of 1774, she renewed her friendship with Turgot. He is said to have proposed marriage a second time, but Madame preferred a platonic relationship.

At Auteuil, Madame resumed her practice of hosting events. These were attended by her husband's friends, Freemasons and others interested in her husband's Science of Man, and men like Turgot, whose investigations encompassed progress in all fields of knowledge. Turgot appears to have brought Cabanis to one of these events after Cabanis began his studies with Dr. Dubreuil. By some accounts, Cabanis successfully treated one of Madame's maladies. In any case, she was charmed by the young *médecin.* By the summer of 1778, Cabanis had moved his residence to a pavilion in the garden behind her home.

Cabanis' housemate, abbé Martin Lefebvre de la Roche, would soon become the literary executor and editor of the papers of Madame's husband. The young medical vitalist used the opportunity to explore Monsieur's theories of Sensation and Utility. Abbé La Roche might have contrasted Monsieur's work with that of Scottish philosopher David Hume whose *A Treatise of Human Nature: Being an Attempt to Introduce the Experimental Method of Reasoning into Moral Subjects* appeared in 1739. The analysis of the Scottish empiricist explicated "the science of man" in terms of Human Nature. Helvétius's great work was a new rendering of this subject. Monsieur's treatise analyzed the sensation of pleasure, how it affected human behavior, and how it could be used to reform society.

As a physiologist, Cabanis was attentive to the way Helvétius connected physical sensitivity and mental sensation in his explanation of human behavior. As an attending physician and steward of the public's health, he was also attentive to Helvétius's recommendations for managing behavior to improve conditions for men in society. Cabanis was sufficiently impressed by Helvétius's ingenious derivation of a principle of morality from pleasurable sensations to incorporate it into his own scheme. In this regard, he followed the prevailing trend.

In his great work, Madame's husband undertook to create a "science", which connected human behavior with morally right behavior. This must have intrigued Cabanis since it was a theme in his vitalist view of Medicine. During conversations with abbé la Roche, sometimes joined by Madame's part time tenant, abbé Morellet, Cabanis acquired a comprehensive understanding of Helvétius's theory and became Helvétius's disciple.

Helvétius built his social science on the materialist premise Locke applied in *Essay Concerning Human Understanding:* physical sensitivity is the causal source of all mental and moral activity. Helvétius advanced beyond Locke by claiming that even the capacities to learn and to manipulate ideas (aptitude and intelligence) are products of eternal sensations. His claim that the fundamental law of human behavior is the search for pleasurable sensations provided the foundation for his heretical analysis of right behavior.

Because intelligence and virtues are products of experience rather than natural aptitudes, Helvétius argued, society can be improved through a state-supported system of education. Right behavior can be inculcated even in the lowest minds by reinforcing moral instruction with pleasurable sensations. In this way, Helvétius made pleasure seeking—self-love—central aspects of morality and social reform. Progressives in Jefferson's Paris agreed that training "the people" to find pleasure in socially constructive ways was vital for perfecting their society.

Not long after Cabanis took up residence in Madame's garden house, Turgot brought Benjamin Franklin to meet her. This marked the beginning of a celebrated relationship between the homespun American sage and the idiosyncratic French hostess, which culminated in a bathtub scene in the HBO TV mini-series *John Adams* (2008). Cabanis' association with Madame facilitated his own uniquely close relationship with "Papa" Franklin.

Franklin recruited Cabanis into the Lodge of the Nine Sisters a few months after his election as its Venerated Master. He served in this post for two years: May 1779 to May 1781. Cabanis did not follow Franklin into the leadership of this celebrated lodge, but his Masonic connections were no doubt useful during his ascent into the hierarchy of French Medicine. The Montpellier Vitalist movement was led by Freemasons. Among these were Paul-Joseph Barthaz, Théophile de Bordeu, and Jean-Antoine Chaptal, all of whom would have known Cabanis. Paul Victor de Seze, who received his medical training in Montpellier, was Cabanis' lodge brother. Cabanis introduced another *médecin Montepelliers,* Philippe Pinel, into his society at Auteuil.

Cabanis is remembered today as the co-founder of a branch of science called *Ideology.* He commenced this enterprise several years after Jefferson's departure form France. Cabanis' friend Destutt de Tracy coined the term in the mid-1790s to refer to the "science of ideas."

A political economist, Tracy was more concerned with the prosperity of society at large than he was about the mental processes of its individual members. For Cabanis, whose spadework prepared the field, the science of ideas encompassed the bodily mechanisms of thought. Part physiology and part psychology, it rested on Locke's mechanistic philosophy of Mind (1690) and on the materialist epistemology Étienne Bonnot de Condilliac presented in his *Essai sur l'origine des connaissances humaines* (1746).

Cabanis' connections with Turgot, with France's energetic society of philosophical doctors, with Madame Helvétius and her husband's philosophy, with Benjamin Franklin, and with the progressive elements of France's Masonic brotherhood gave him a network of associates that even Condorcet would been hard pressed to match.

Unlike the leisure class members of this network, Cabanis was a professional trained and inclined to apply the Science of Man. During his training, Cabanis developed skills for analyzing concepts in terms of overarching theories and for defending them against competitive theories and concepts. He did all of these things in the context of his mentor's innovative vision of man in society. For Cabanis, the science he was promoting contributed to the perfection of society in the great march of human progress. When Jefferson reached France, these ideas were fueling a broad-based reform movement in which Cabanis was a prominent and instrumental figure.

chapter fourteen

Cabanis' Program

*J*efferson waited for Pilippe-Denis Pierres to print his book before embarking into Parisian society. When Madame d'Houdetot invited him to dinner several weeks later, he announced the fact to Abigail Adams. He hoped, he confessed in his 21 June 1785 letter, that it would gain him admittance to "the circle of literati with which she is environed." In other words, he was not yet part of it.

The fact that he made no corresponding mention of dining with Madame Helvétius suggests to me that he had nothing to report in this department. Franklin took Abigail Adams to meet her without forewarning la Notre Dame d'Auteuil. Evidently he did even less for the man who would soon replace him. Although it is commonly accepted that Jefferson socialized with Franklin's "sultaness", the connection does not appear to have been close. When and where they met is not part of the written record.

I expect Jefferson met Madame's dearest companion (after her lapdog Pompon) before he made her acquaintance. The likeliest place for *une rencontre fortuite* would have been Franklin's residence in Passy. Both men visited Franklin there. I believe the opening event in Jefferson's enlightenment took place there when Jefferson encountered Pierre Cabanis for the first time.

Franklin's association with Cabanis began in the fall of 1778. Between then and Jefferson's arrival in the August of 1784, an unusual friendship developed between the two men. Their fondness for each other can be seen in their letters. In one that Cabanis sent Franklin as a 23-year old, he referred to himself as "your little son". In a letter Franklin sent on June 30, 1780, he told his boy that "I long for your return". Franklin's paternal sentiments seem to have been rooted in qualities of Cabanis' person that allowed him to perform two intimate services. He served as an intermediary between the randy old American and the coy French maven. He also supplied the crafty homespun with tidbits of useful information and wise counsel.

Somewhere along the way, Franklin mentioned to Cabanis that his replacement had been involved in drafting the *Declaration of Independence*. Cabanis could have easily have gotten a copy. (The duc de la Rochefoucauld published one of the first, if not the first, translations in a 1777 issue of *Affaires de l'Angleterre et de l'Amérique*. Franklin probably had more than one copy of it. The duc published another copy in his 1783 book *Constitutions des treize Etats-Unis de l'Amérique,* which Franklin helped edit.) While reading the document, Cabanis would have noticed that the opening appeals to Natural Law and Natural Right were approximations of concepts John Locke had invoked in his *Second Treatise of Government.* He would also have noticed that nowhere in the document were the central concepts of the Enlightenment in France identified or referenced.

Although its roots were in the English minds of Isaac Newton and John Locke, the French Enlightenment was not like the

Enlightenment in England. Enlightenment in France grew out of Locke's theory of Mind, not his advocacy for religious tolerance or majoritarian government. Eighteenth century French philosophes were mesmerized by Locke's characterization of the human mind as a *tabula rasa,* which gradually filled with data provided by sensory experience. To think, for Locke and his French followers, was a mechanical process in which data are combined and contrasted. As this idea rippled through French science, the natural world transformed into a Newtonian mechanism.

By mid-century, this way of seeing the world was becoming embedded in a view of man in society, which combined the material with the moral. When Jefferson arrived in France, the Science of Man, with its branch into utilitarian ethics, was accepted as an instrument for perfecting society and advancing the great march of human progress. By then, the enterprise had solidified into an impending movement that was concerned with every aspect of France's backward, degenerate society. Cabanis was part of this movement. These were the essential concepts that underpinned it: Mind, Reason, Progress, the Perfectibility of Man and Society, and Education.

Cabanis understood that the argument in the preamble of a declaration of political independence would not say much about the connection between thought and sensation. This did not keep him from feeling disappointment that the American *Declaration of Independence* had not even a trace of Turgot's concept of progress or his view mankind's perfectibility. Nor did it allude to Helvétius's concept of utility or his enlightened thesis that moral education would improve the well-being of individuals and society in general.

When they met, Cabanis was struck by Jefferson's dissimilarity to Franklin. Franklin was avuncular. Jefferson was aloof. Franklin was comfortable. Jefferson was correct. Franklin was rambling. Jefferson was on point. Franklin was a man of the world. Jefferson was not. In their brief exchange, Cabanis took the trouble to inquire whether Jefferson had referred to Locke while preparing his draft of the *Declaration of Independence*. The answer had been no. Asked his opinion on Locke's *Essay*, Jefferson had no opinion—he had never heard of it. As a physician trained to evaluate the health of his patients, Cabanis found Jefferson's symptoms disquieting. Here was an intelligent man, who lacked both the social grace and the store of knowledge necessary to prosper in French society.

The man who offered his hand that day was fourteen years younger than Jefferson. He had been part of Madame Helvétius's household for six years. The secular cleric who shared his residence had lived there since Madame acquired the property seven years before that.

The year before he met Jefferson, Cabanis completed his medical studies and paid his licensing fees. The new Doctor of Medicine had an analytical mind that had blossomed as he wended his way through the curriculum of *le médecins philosophes* of Montpellier. During the five years he spent in this endeavor, Cabanis mastered a tangle of theories that spread across the two millennia from Hippocrates to John Locke's 18th century sensationalist disciples.

The concepts that underpinned the ancient art of medicine were now being modernized and treatment of human illness was improving dramatically. Men like Cabanis were both theorists and practitioners. This "medical philosopher" would later revamp the training of all doctors in Paris.

His father's friend from Limoges took Cabanis under his wing and became his advocate after Cabanis committed himself to the service of humanity. Cabanis had known Turgot when he was a small child. But little Pierre had known nothing of the revolutionary theory Turgot unveiled as a lecturer at the Sorbonne. Nor did he understand the economic principles Turgot applied as Intendant of Limoges. Not until he was a teenager in Poland did Cabanis become acquainted with these things or notice that they were ingenious.

Because they were connected through Prince-Bishop Massalski to the affairs of Poland's new education commission, Cabanis and du Pont de Nemours became acquainted. Being countrymen with similar assignments, they were drawn to each other. Added to this was the intangible factor that du Pont liked to talk. When Cabanis mentioned his childhood in Limoges, du Pont responded by remembering his connections with Turgot, which opened conversation to Turgot's ideas and methods.

Again in Paris, Cabanis located a copy and read Turgot's celebrated discourse, "On the successive Advances of the Human Mind." Praised for being "one of the earliest enunciations of the perfectibility of the human race," it connected Cabanis with the idea that propelled the French Enlightenment into the reform movement that was gaining momentum when Jefferson arrived. By then, Cabanis was one of its respected advocates.

The first door Turgot opened for his protégé led into the circle of *philosophes* and *literati* who gathered at the home of his ancient friend in Auteuil. Turgot met "Minette" de Ligniville during his school days. When Pierre met her three decades later, Madame was cultivating a new circle of cosmopolitans. Some apt medical advice may have cemented the bond between them. In the summer of 1778, the physician-in-training left his lodging near the hospital in Saint-Germain-en-Laye and entered Madame's household.

In the company of Helvétius's literary executor, Cabanis investigated Helvétius's application of Turgot's concept of human perfectibility. If right behavior produces social harmony and personal happiness, and if the inclination to be virtuous can be instilled through public education, then society can perfect itself by implementing right policies. As a scientist versed in the physiology of this progressive view, Cabanis played a constructive role in Madame's gatherings and in the network he was building with her help and the help of Turgot.

The man who scrutinized Jefferson that day in Franklin's quarters was a progressive. His worldview was rooted in the conviction that progress was a moral imperative. All the best men (his friends) shared this conviction. But there was more to it. After years of tireless encouragement from the great Franklin, all of them had come to see the revolution in America as the confirmation of their hope-filled view of the world. America was the fulfillment of their enlightened reforms, the perfection to which progress led.

In this fabric of thought, Cabanis found the American revolutionary interestingly incomplete. This was awkward since the untraveled Virginian would soon be America's agent in France. In deference to Franklin, Cabanis resolved to intervene. He would bring the new American envoy into the French Enlightenment. He would make Jefferson like the others in his enlightened circle.

Transforming the savage from the American mountains into a progressive cosmopolitan would not be easy. Cabanis spent years studying and reflecting. He had been tutored by some of France's most remarkable men. How would he impart such a complex system of knowledge to someone who did not even speak the language? The best he could do, Cabanis decided, would be to seed the field. He would show Jefferson through the French capital and acquaint him with its history. Perhaps they would enjoy each other's company. If so, he would venture into a deeper discussion.

Jefferson had not circulated far through the world of ideas so there was no telling what he knew about the intellectual revolution that had been changing Europe for the past hundred years. Cabanis decided to begin with a few comments about the man who launched it. John Adcock had composed a poem to honor Isaac Newton after the publication of his famous treatise, *Philosophiae Naturalis Principia Mathematica*. It went like this:

Greek logic could never explain

The problem of stasis and change,
So the sage proved the notion
That laws govern motion.
Thus enlightened the world rearranged.

Cabanis would speak on this theme. By referencing works of a few Newtonian pioneers, he would show Jefferson how the science of Nature (in which the observable world is a continuum of systems governed by empirically discoverable laws) replaced the philosophy of Nature (in which the natures of things are revealed by discerning their Aristotelian essences).

He would describe how freethinking English non-conformists transformed John Locke's appeals for religious tolerance into an assault on the orthodoxies of the Christian faith, and how this was the beginning of a relationship between man and God based on reason. He would make the point that the Age of Reason dawned in England.

He would observe that the path away from Dark Age superstition led from England to Scotland where reasonable men discovered Natural Religion. It was in Scotland that enlightened cosmopolitans coined the idea that actions are right if they are compatible with the interests of the community. This concept—Utility—provided the cornerstone for a *philosophy* of Morality (in which right behavior is determined through the application of human reason). It was in Scotland that the Moral *theology* of Medieval schoolmen (in which right behavior is the Will of God revealed in Scripture) ceased to be a topic of serious conversation. Cabanis would note that the

Enlightenment in Scotland differed from the English Dawn. It was a metamorphosis of Morality.

He would point out that *philosophes* in France did not become acquainted with Newton's analytical method until Voltaire recommended it in 1734 and that a French translation of his magnum opus was not made until Madame du Châtelet produced one in 1749. Two years later, Diderot published the first volume of an encyclopedia filled with Newtonian investigations into the nature of all things. The Enlightenment in France was therefore like unto itself – as it had been in England and Scotland. In France, it was marked by the apotheosis of Reason as a light for understanding men in Nature.

After pointing out that the Enlightenment was a sequence of different events, Cabanis would focus on a few of its pivotal episodes in France: how French thinkers, having harnessed Locke's Science of Mind, were using it to in a reform movement that would perfect French society. He would acknowledge Montesquieu's effort to demystify the laws that govern society by explaining them in terms of the physical conditions in which societies form and function. He would refer to Voltaire's rebellion against the Catholic Church and explain how Voltaire's incisive critiques about the corruptions of the French monarchy had shaped opinion to favor change. He would explain how the materialist philosophies of Condillac and Holbach provided a bridge from Locke's Science of Mind to Helvétius's Science of Man. He would introduce Quesnay and du Pont and show Jefferson how their quantitative analyzes had been used to modernize and grow France's backward economy. Rousseau had long ago fallen out with Cabanis' salon friends, but his commentaries on social equality remained fundamental to their reform movement.

The centering theme in Cabanis' program was the presentation of these enlightened initiatives in terms of his mentor's concept of the Perfectibility of Man. Turgot's ingenious concept gave knowledge derived from investigations in Newtonian science positive direction and value. This knowledge allowed men to improve the quality of their lives as they promoted their common good. Cabanis would introduce Jefferson to Turgot's brilliant friend. The marquis de Condorcet was crystalizing this tendency into a general principle, a Doctrine of Progress.

As Cabanis conceptualized his program, he realized that he must learn from Jefferson how America was developing in the wake of its revolution. America's Enlightenment was following a course different from what it was in England, in Scotland, and in France. If the French Enlightenment grew out of Locke's Theory of Mind into a reform movement, perhaps the Enlightenment in American should be cast as a reform movement inspired by Locke's Theory of Government. If he could confirm this, perhaps Cabanis would be able to anticipate how the revolution in America would impact the reform movement in his own country. As this thought crossed his mind, he realized that he was going to enjoy his adventure with Jefferson.

chapter fifteen

Jefferson's Transformation

I believe the transformation that Thomas Jefferson experienced during his sojourn in France occurred in two phases, the second being more significant than the first.

In its first phase, young French physician Pierre Cabanis acquainted Jefferson with the city of Paris, the dire circumstances of France's monarchy and people, and the enlightened ideas that motivated the Frenchmen had undertaken to reform its Mediaeval society. Jefferson applied what he learned in this propaedeutic to attire himself and his home in French fashions, to stock a gentleman's library, and to become conversant in matters interesting to men and women who communed in the salons of Paris. Unlike his instructor, however, Jefferson did not use his library to explore in the realm of ideas. The books he purchased, like his furniture, paintings, and drapes, remained in their assigned places while Jefferson launched into the second phase of his transformation.

Cabanis, like Papa Franklin, orbited in several Parisian solar systems. His network of connections included virtually all the *illuminati* in the French capital. I believe it was Cabanis, not Franklin, who introduced Jefferson to these celestial bodies. Each, Jefferson discovered, was engaged in a different facet of societal reform. Members of Madame Helvétius's circle were advancing knowledge in fields of science. Members of Madame d'Houdetot's circle were debating the value of public education and other programs to ameliorate the condition of the poor. Members of duchesse d'Anville's circle were exploring ways to make French agriculture more productive and to modernize its economy. Parisian Masonic lodges, filled with men from these elite circles, were improving society by teaching men of good will progressive principles of benevolence and public virtue.

During the immersion phase of his enlightenment, Jefferson met the duc de la Rochefoucauld and the "chateau reformers" in his elite circle. These men were prominent advocates in a quiet effort to replace France's bankrupt monarchy with a constitutional government. Ironically, while they were leaders in this hopeful enterprise, they knew little about constitutional government or the nature of the rights of man on which it rested. When Jefferson entered this circle, he became its reigning expert on these lofty matters. As conditions deteriorated during the two years prior to the storming of the Bastille, the duc and his confreres turned increasingly to Jefferson for advice on these matters. Flattered and encouraged by their deference to his opinions, Jefferson pulled back his veil and began, at last, to speak his mind. Jefferson's engagement with the members of the duc's progressive circle marked the completion of his transformation. The circumspect political loner had become an engaged reform-minded progressive.

Jefferson shared the views of the others in the duc's progressive circle in respect to the monarchy's approaching bankruptcy. Instead of fearing the impending collapse, they welcomed it as an opportunity to implement the reforms they advocated. Having no alternative, in the fall of 1787, the King called an Estates General to convene the following spring. Prior to its opening, political activists in Paris began to develop their ideas for a new constitutional government. As these deliberations proceeded, what Turgot had warned against in 1774 occurred. On 16 August 1788, the royal treasury defaulted on the king's massive debts and the government descended into bankruptcy.

Jefferson had ended his self-imposed isolation in the late spring of 1785. When he entered French society he left the Wizard of Oz in his closet at home. Now, ironically, he was asked to return into his Patriotic shadow and retrieve the ideas he had crystalized as the circumspect political loner. The newly enlightened progressive would go on to distinguish himself in France by preaching the gospels of the American Revolution, not by applying themes of enlightened French thought.

In my account, Cabanis diagnosed Jefferson's social disorder during their first interview. Pinpointing the problem as a deficiency in the art of social fluency, the physician devised a program to improve his patient's circulation. Since the aristocratic Virginian had no philo-sophical curiosity or conversation, Cabanis resolved to dose him with information. He failed to discern, however, that Jefferson considered speculation a waste of time and conscientiously avoided it. The doctor's prescription was beneficial for worldly men in late-18th century France who prospered socially according to their ability to apply abstract idea as instruments of progress. How Jefferson would respond to the treatment was unknowable.

When Cabanis described his plan to Franklin, the American Ambassador arranged another meeting between the doctor and his unsuspecting patient. During this encounter, the Frenchman broached his proposition: would Jefferson participate in an exchange of knowledge? What knowledge would that be, the judicious American wondered. Cabanis would share his insights in respect to French manners and society for Jefferson's insights on the American Revolution and the progress of American society under republican government.

Jefferson brought with him to France two valuable assets. The first was his experience as a penman for the American Independence Party. (He knew from speaking with Chastellux at Monticello that enlightened Frenchmen viewed the revolution as a consequential event.) In addition to this, he had his book about Virginia. Assuming that his opinions on subjects relating to these topics would interest France's cognoscenti, Jefferson accepted Cabanis' proposal and agreed to meet him at a place Cabanis thought fitting.

In my reconstruction, their first excursion takes place after Jefferson received his books from Philippe-Denis Pierres in May 1785. Their last outing takes place in September, not long after Jefferson's first visit to the duc de la Rochefoucauld at la Roche-Guyon. As Jefferson became involved with the enterprise of the duc and his circle, Cabanis shifted his attention to evaluating the city's plan for new 5,400-bed hospital.

During June, July, and August of 1785, the two men passed several enjoyable hours touring the city, inspecting Parisian architecture, and sharing conversations about the French Enlightenment and the American Revolution. I portray both men in character. Cabanis plies his companion with an unending stream of information. Jefferson files bits of it away for future reference, but mostly he listens and observes how his host comports himself.

My reconstruction of Jefferson's enlightenment begins in the **le Jardin des Tuileries.** One bright June morning, Jefferson meets Cabanis in the plaza between the Louvre and the Tuileries Palace. The genial Frenchman leads his companion through a passage in the palace and onto the garden's central promenade. The ingeniousness of the garden's design stimulates conversation.

Cabanis describes how his medical training carried him into the history of ideas. He comments on his connection with Madame Helvétius and his friendship with Franklin. Jefferson describes his earlier activities with the Ambassador and the influence the marquis de Chastellux exerted in his decision to come to France. While relating the history of the gardens, Cabanis is pleased to find that Jefferson too is a gardener and intends one day to create a *ferme orne* on the grounds of his estate in central Virginia.

As they chat, Cabanis is careful to comment on the importance of Isaac Newton's scientific revolution. Jefferson makes no response to this. The points Cabanis is making are that celestial bodies move according to discoverable "natural" laws and Newton's demonstration changed what had been a collection of Aristotelian forms into a machine. Thoughtful men everywhere responded to Newton's discovery by launching investigations of their own.

Locke was one of these men, Cabanis explains. The Theory of Mind he presented in his *Essay Concerning on Human Understanding* is the second great building block in France's *éclaircissement*. Jefferson listens as Cabanis recounts how Locke performed a Newtonian examination of what takes place when the human mind processes a thought. Enlightened Frenchmen, he observes, agree that the human mind processes data provided by the senses. Jefferson nods. Cabanis concludes by observing that threads of Lockean sensationalism have been woven into virtually every branch of French science.

On their next excursion, the two men meet on rue de Richelieu. Cabanis then leads Jefferson into the arcades of **le Palais Royal**. This is the "brain of the city" and one of the few places in Paris where individuals from all its social strata mingle. Cabanis uses the occasion to acquaint the unschooled American with the men who began enlightening France fifty years before.

François-Marie Arouet, Voltaire, exiled himself to England the year before Newton's death. Although he did not meet the great man, he met the great man's sister who told him the story of the inspiring apple that dropped on her brother's head. Cabanis notes that Voltaire's *Lettres philosophiques* (1734) provided French readers with their first admiring accounts of Newton, Locke, and Bacon. He points out that Voltaire was a social critic, not a scientist, and that he needed help from his brilliant lover, Emilie Le Tonnier de Breteuil, the marquise du Châtelet, to prepare the first French translation of Newton's celebrated work. Voltaire's objective in publishing her book, *Éléments de la Philosophie de Newton,* Cabanis explains, was to build a following in France for the Newton's scientific method of discovery. Jefferson listens politely.

Cabanis distinguishes Charles-Louis de Secondat, baron de La Brède et de Montesquieu from Voltaire, noting that the baron was a scientist. He became aware of Newton while visiting England in the late 1720s. So impressed was he that he resolved to undertake a Newtonian investigation of his own to establish the laws that govern the operation of societies and their institutions.

Cabanis makes these comments in the course of an exploration that takes the two men to Dr. Curtius' famous wax works and to the Café Maçonnique where Cabanis introduces Jefferson to the aeronauts who use the mechanical coffeehouse as their headquarters. Most of these men are Freemasons. In fact, Cabanis explains, the *palais* is the center of Freemasonry in Paris. Cabanis is himself a Mason. Jefferson is not, and he explains why. At the *palais,* Jefferson sees the commercial, social, and political sides of Parisian life.

In their third excursion, the two men cross Pont Neuf and travel down rue Dauphine to rue de Conde at rue de Vaugirard. This is the location of **le Théâtre-Français** where they attend the 90th performance of *The Marriage of Figaro.* In the audience are more that 1500 members of the city's bourgeoisie. They are there, Cabanis explains, to acquire culture and to improve themselves. Their presence, Cabanis opines, illustrates the broad reach of France's Enlightenment.

Cabanis credits Denis Diderot for this. Jefferson does not know him. Cabanis describes Diderot as a self-appointed Ambassador of Reason. His mission, Cabanis explains, was to modernize the Arts and to deliver the people of France—and men everywhere—from the tyranny of organized religion. Jefferson expresses his supports for the enterprise. After the performance, Cabanis takes him to the Café Procope where they drink champagne and trade bon mots with the man who wrote the play. Beaumarchais explains why he risked his fortune to support the American rebellion against England. The prospect of establishing government by the people did not motivate him, Beaumarchais explains. Nor was he inspired by idea that the American Revolution was a step forward in the march of human progress. He acted because it was in the interests of France and because he admired the audacity of men who would risk their lives, their fortunes, and their honor to govern themselves. The affair becomes awkward when he shares his opinions about the men who are refusing to pay him for the supplies they received.

A fourth meeting takes place at Jefferson's hôtel in **cul de sac Taitbout.** Cabanis arrives unannounced to congratulate the new American Ambassador on his appointment as Franklin's replacement.

Jefferson and Cabanis are joined by Jefferson's secretary. William Short has recently affiliated with Cabanis' Masonic lodge. Settling themselves in the gardened patio beside the Ambassador's office,

they fall into a rambling conversation. Cabanis informs his companions that they have been invited to attend a gathering at the townhome of Jefferson's admirer, Madame d'Houdetot. Cabanis comments
on a few of the men and women who commune in Madame's salon.
Cabanis' friend and fellow Americaniste, the duc la Rochefoucauld,
sometimes attends. He is the key to Jefferson's future in France, the
Frenchman opines. The key to the duc's door, he continues, is held
by a man who is difficult to impress. Jefferson wonders who this
man is. The marquis de Condorcet. Jefferson does not know him.

Cabanis explains that the duc and his friends think that the future
of France depends on reconstituting its government. Jefferson
wonders whether they are followers of Montesquieu, whom he has
read. Cabanis shrugs and returns to a point he made earlier about
the connection between the French Enlightenment and John Locke's
Theory of Mind. Madame Helvétius's husband is the link between
John Locke and the reforms the duc and the marquis seek, Cabanis
explains. He asks if Jefferson is familiar with the concept of Utility.
Jefferson shakes his head. Utility, Cabanis explains, is a rational
account of right behavior: what is morally correct is that which
produces the greatest good for the greatest number. He notes the
connection between Helvétius's theory and Jefferson's Happiness
Principle. Jefferson nods. Because of Monsieur's genius, Cabanis
concludes, progress is a moral imperative.

Cabanis reaches into his valise and extracts a copy of Adam
Smith's *Wealth of Nations,* which he hands to Jefferson. Jefferson
must also familiarize himself with the science of *Oeconomics,*

Cabanis announces. The duc and the marquis are both keen on it. Jefferson hands his guest a copy of his little book. Cabanis is delighted. To repay the author's kindness, Cabanis reveals that du Pont de Nemours authored the questions Jefferson has answered in it.

Their fifth event takes place at **Madame d'Houdetot's Salon,** which Jefferson and his secretary reach after a brisk twenty-minute walk from the Ambassador's residence. Cabanis meets the two men as they arrive and takes them to meet their hostess. Madame expresses her delight in an effusive greeting then silences the room so Jefferson can speak. He said exactly the right things, Cabanis assures him afterward. Jefferson and his hostess then greet her guests.

The Ambassador accepts many compliments and trades friendly comments with a number of admirers. One of these is the duc de la Rochefoucauld. Cabanis whispers that he will introduce Jefferson to Condorcet when he finishes his duty in the reception line. On their way to meet the prickly philosophe, they are intercepted by the man Cabanis described at le Hôtel Landron, France's leading economist, du Pont de Nemours. Du Pont is typically disheveled and bubbling with emotion. His joy upon meeting Jefferson is beyond restraint. The Ambassador wants to speak with the man who knows how to make farms productive and countries wealthy, but their conversation must wait until another day. Jefferson invites du Pont to come to his office the following week. Meeting Condorcet is the current priority. Jefferson finds the marquis intimidating, but he departs from their brief meeting with an invitation to call on the imposing philosophe.

In their sixth excursion, Cabanis takes Jefferson for a weekend retreat at **le Hermitage des Mount Valerian.** Their destination is across the Seine west of Paris. Cabanis intends to prepare the American for his interview with the marquis. If Jefferson does well, Cabanis expects that he will be invited to join the duc's small circle. Cabanis plans a review that will extend across a wide range of subjects. During their coach ride, he extracts from his valise one book after another. Each explicates a scientific theory or a philosophical concept that Condorcet admires.

Among the political sciences are works by Locke and Montesquieu. Cabanis has also brought Rousseau's *Discourse on the Origin of Inequality* (1754) and *Social Contract or Principles of Political Right* (1662). He makes a special point of opening *le Constitutions des treize États-Unis de l'Amérique* to the duc's translation of Jefferson's *Declaration of Independence.* Among his texts on the science of economics are several by Quesnay including his *Tableau économique.* Of course he also has Adam Smith's *An Inquiry into the Nature and Causes of the Wealth of Nations,* and Turgot's *Reflections on the Formation and the Distribution of Riches* (1770), and Rousseau's *Discourse on Political Economy* (1755).

Regarding the science of progress, Cabanis shows Jefferson Turgot's *The History of the Progress of the Human Mind* (1750). He has a manuscript for *la Vie de Monsieur Turgot,* which he is editing for Condorcet. Cabanis becomes animated as he pulls out another dog-eared manuscript, *Essai sur l'application de l'analyse à la probabilité des décisions rendues à la pluralité des voix (Essay on the*

Application of Analysis to the Probability of Majority Decisions). The marquis claims to have devised a way to determine how often majorities are right in their opinions! Cabanis marvels at the idea. Are they ever? Jefferson quips.

Of all the texts Cabanis has with him, this next one is the most important. Jefferson leans forward and gazes at a document in draft form. It contains the outline for marquis' great treatise. Cabanis refers to it as a picture of the progress of the human spirit. Of all the things Condorcet will want to know from Jefferson, Cabanis warns, the first will be whether Jefferson agrees with him on the conditions necessary for republican government to succeed. It is all here, Cabanis declares. This will be the primary focus of their weekend review. What is it about? Jefferson asks, taking the text and tumbling through it. It is the marquis' Doctrine of Progress.

Not long after introducing Jefferson to the marquis de Corndorcet's Doctrine of Progress, Cabanis escorts his pupil to **le Hôtel des Monnaies** to speak with the man. I put the two men into a conversation to show that while Jefferson has not mastered the art of conceptual analysis, he is able to stand his ground against an assault by France's greatest thinker. Having passed the marquis' little test, Condorcet takes the American republican into his confidence. He explains that the French government is bankrupt, that the French economy is being strangled, and that France's hierarchical social system is a breeding ground for corruption and human suffering.

But the real problem, the marquis announces, is that twenty four million men and women in France can neither read, write, nor reason. What will happen, he asks Jefferson, if we give them your political rights?

Jefferson has spent his time in Paris preparing to join its thinking class. As much as possible, he has avoided the filthy people who clog the city's streets. The idea that they would become a political majority and decide policy is something he has never considered. As he ponders the matter, he realizes that all eyes are on him. The marquis breaks the silence. "What shall we do?" Jefferson glances at Cabanis who gives an imperceptible shrug. "Je ne sais pas," Jefferson says at last. The marquis stiffens. "You must think of something." With this brazen command, Condorcet welcomes Jefferson into the sanctum sanctorum of France's elite.

Having passed the marquis' test, Jefferson enters the duc's circle. Cabanis has time for one final excursion. This is to **la Halle aux Blés** in the market district not far from Jefferson's residence. Cabanis takes Jefferson there to see common people working. He has asked one of France's new men, Jacques Pierre Brissot de Warville, to meet them there. Cabanis admits that Brissot is better acquainted with these people than he is.

Brissot is a writer, which means that he lives by his wits. He informs the American Ambassador that his business is politics and that he needs information from Jefferson. What is it? Jefferson wonders. Brissot and his cohorts are organizing to overthrow the monarchy and replace it with a government by the people. Jefferson is shocked. They intend to follow the same program Jefferson and his compatriots did, Brissot observes. Jefferson is nonplussed. Yes, Brissot continues, we will turn the people against the king. Jefferson wonders what they are going got do to ameliorate the suffering of the people. Brissot shrugs. That was not the purpose of the revolution in America, Brissot observes. My cohorts and I will wage the same revolution you did – for the same reason.

They intend to run the government and make the law. But they are missing an important piece of knowledge. What would that be? Jefferson wonders. Brissot and his compatriots wish to know how Jefferson and his compatriots coordinated the activities of their insurgents.

My purpose in bringing Jefferson into this tense conversation is five fold:

1) to show that France's best and brightest men were not the only ones conspiring to change France's government,

2) to show that although France's intelligentsia was filled with brilliant individuals, they did not control its political impulses,

3) to show that political outcomes are not decided by genius,

4) to show that in politics good intentions count for relatively little, and

5) to emphasize that political movements are created and managed by men who hunger for power.

I think Jefferson became such a man while he was engaged in reforming France. He became a progressive. As he did, his vision of the common good crystalized. This vision was accompanied by a moral conviction that it is right to do whatever is necessary to accomplish it. When the progressive returned home, the new American President commanded him to take a seat in his first cabinet. As the first Secretary of State for the United States of America, Jefferson initiated a clandestine campaign to turn public opinion against his influential rival, Alexander Hamilton. When it became apparent that he could not diminish the influence Hamilton exerted on the President, Jefferson resigned. Soon after that, he joined the opposition party his friend James Madison was organizing.

When President Washington retired from public life, Jefferson allowed his name to be placed in nomination as a candidate to succeed him. He showed his deference to the wishes of George Washington during the presidential election of 1796 by refusing to campaign. But in the presidential election of 1800, with extensive help from the agents of James Madison's political party, Jefferson waged and won the nation's first national political campaign. This campaign, noted for its negative tone and divisiveness, became a model for office seekers across the country. If there was an Age of Reason in America, this marked its ends. I contend that this brutal contest marked the beginning of the Age of Politics and that the man who learned to be a progressive in France was its leading light.

chapter sixteen

Jefferson as Progressive Theorist

The available information suggests that Jefferson did not begin to circulate in Parisian society until after he finished compiling his notesfrom Virginia into a printable manuscript. He emerged from his seclusion soon after he received the printed copies of his book, which he said he did on 10 May 1785. It was after this, I believe, that he began his four-month cultural immersion with Pierre Cabanis. During their eight excursions, Cabanis prepared the circumspect Virginian to share company with of the best people of Paris.

Jefferson gained his bearings and learned to behave like a late-18th century French cosmopolitan during his time with Cabanis. About six weeks after he began his reconstruction project, Benjamin Franklin returned home and Jefferson was appointed to replace him. The new American Ambassador to France was welcomed into the enlightened circles of the French capital. His little book contained unique information, which he could cite to demonstrate his genius in matters of science. He was less successful in mastering the art of enlightened reasoning. In these next pages, I comment on what is perhaps his most famous attempt at conceptual analysis. It took place in Fontainebleau in October of 1785.

We step back before leaping forward.

Half the entries Jefferson made in the "literary commonplace book" he kept during his student days in Williamsburg are excerpts from the works of Henry St. John, Lord Bolingbroke. Not a single passage that Jefferson copied into his daybook was written by John Locke. The entries he made during his three-year membership in Governor Fauquier's small circle show that he was focused on Religion, not on Philosophy or Politics. This is not surprising since he was beginning his migration away from Anglicanism into Deism and Natural Religion. The surviving record of Jefferson's intellectual development in these formative years does not show the young man analyzing concepts in terms of overarching principles or applying them on behalf of general theses. It shows a schoolboy internalizing points he found salient in the books he was reading.

William Small returned to England in 1762. Before he departed, Jefferson remembered later, he arranged for his prize pupil to read the Law with George Wythe. What Jefferson learned during his five-year study program under Wythe (1762–1767) guided his thinking in the years preceding and through the American Revolution. Under Wythe, Jefferson became expert in legal reasoning and interpreting the Common Law of England. He applied this skill in his first political tract, *A Summary View of the Rights of British America* (1774) in which he presented what I call his "argument from sovereignty". Based on a precedent he found in Saxon law, Jefferson claimed "that the British parliament has no right to exercise authority over us."

That Jefferson continued to reason like a lawyer during the revolutionary era is obscured by what he wrote in the preamble of the *Declaration of Independence.*

The *Declaration of Independence* is remembered for the "argument from right", which appears in its preamble: "all men are endowed by their Creator with certain unalienable Rights, that among these are Life, Liberty, and the pursuit of Happiness . . . that whenever any form of government becomes destructive of these ends, it is the right of the people to alter or abolish it, and to institute new government, laying its foundation on such principles, and organizing its powers in such form, as to them shall seem most likely to effect their safety and happiness." This argument does not rest on a legal precedent. Nor was it Jefferson's. The propositions that all men have Rights by Nature and are authorized to "alter or abolish governments" that violate them was a philosophical argument, which Jefferson and his fellow committeemen borrowed (without attribution) from George Mason's *Virginia Declaration of Rights.*

Back to France and conceptual analysis:

Not long after Jefferson completed Cabanis' introduction to the French Enlightenment, he undertook to test its method of reasoning. In this test run, Jefferson revisited an issue he had argued with the legal logic that guided him from his student days with George Wythe until his adventures with Pierre Cabanis.

In the *Summary View,* Jefferson rejected land tenures on the grounds that they violated Saxon law. "Our Saxon ancestors," he argued, "held their lands, as they did their personal property, in absolute dominion, disencumbered with any superior, answering nearly to the nature of those possessions which the feudalists term allodial." This legal precedent underpinned the right Jefferson extended in his Constitution for the State of Virginia: "Lands held heretofore of the crown in feesimple, and those hereafter to be appropriated shall be holden in full and absolute dominion, of no superior whatever." But in his 28 October 1785 letter to Madison, Jefferson framed the issue in this strikingly new way:

> Whenever there are in any country uncultivated lands and unemployed poor, **it is clear that the laws of property have been so far extended as to violate natural right.** [Emphasis added] The earth is given as a common stock for man to labor and live on. If for the encouragement of industry we allow it to be appropriated, we must take care that other employment be provided to those excluded from the appropriation. If we do not, the fundamental right to labor the earth returns to the unemployed.

In this claim, Jefferson applied a concept that was commonplace among his enlightened new acquaintances. They had read Locke and knew that it was Locke who originally framed it. He had done this a decade before he published his *Second Treatise of Government* (1689). Locke used it to introduce his argument on behalf of political Majoritarianism. In Paragraph 25 of his *Second Treatise,* he announced, "I shall endeavor to show how men might come to have a property in several parts of that which God gave mankind in common." Locke published his treatise as William of Orange was wrapping up Parliament's rebellion against James II. His purpose in doing so was to justify a "popular" revolution against an authoritarian King. In his treatise, Locke defended government by the will of the majority against the rule of an absolutist monarch on the grounds that the majority of a society's body politic has a right by nature to define their common good and to approve their laws.

Jean-Jacques Rousseau published his second treatise, entitled *Discourse on the Origin and Basis of Inequity Among Men,* sixty-six years after Locke published his *Second Treatise of Government.* The French *philosophe* opened his essay with the claim that "the fruits of the earth belong to us all, and the earth itself to nobody."

Social leveling, which is to say dismantling feudalism, had been under way in England for nearly a century when Rousseau published his second treatise. It was being fueled by revolutions in agricultural and industry and the commerce they stimulated. During this time, France made no appreciable social progress. Its medieval agrarian system, with its land tenures and institutionalized servitude, continued to hold the French masses in destitution.

Rousseau's paper put him in the front line of a broad assault on the economically stifling system that underpinned this massive social injustice. Jacques Claude Marie Vincent de Gournay had launched the enterprise two decades before Rousseau joined it. François Quesnay and Anne-Robert-Jacques Turgot carried it on through the end of the 1770s when the marquis de Condorcet and du Pont de Nemours became its leading proponents. Adam Smith was leading a parallel effort in the British Isles. Among the landed gentry in colonial Virginia, Jefferson was one of the few—perhaps the only one—to see a problem with land tenures.

The aspiring American may have heard Rousseau's name for the first time at one of Madame d'Houdetot's gatherings. Reformers in the enlightened Parisian circles were philosophically disposed to endorse Rousseau's progressive social agenda, but they were culturally unprepared to associate with Rousseau's petit bourgeoisie constituents. The civic-minded commitment of France's chateau reformers to reform their backward society drew them instead to the physiocratic economics of Quesnay and Turgot and to the *laissez-faire* philosophy of Adam Smith.

Jefferson seems to have followed his enlightened friends in keeping Rousseau at arm's length. In Adam Smith, however, he found a kindred spirit. Smith, who died in 1790, was one of Franklin's confreres and on friendly terms with the leading reformers in pre-revolutionary France. I suggest that Jefferson heard his name for the first time from Cabanis. Jefferson acquired a copy of *The Wealth of Nations* at this time. I suggest that Cabanis gave it to him with instructions on the sections he should read.

Smith concluded his three-part inquiry into the nature and causes of the wealth of nations with a section titled "Of the Different Progress of Opulence in Different Nations." The French themes in this section show the impact France's leading *philosophes* and *physiocrats* had on Smith's thinking. (He spent several months communing with them in Paris before returning home later in 1766.) Smith's discussions on the "wantonness of plenty", the economic relationship between towns and the country that surrounds them, the relationship between agriculture and commerce, and "how the towns improve the country," all followed French themes. These comments are all found under the header, "The Discouragement of Agriculture." Also in this section are Smith's observations concerning the problems of Primogeniture and Entailment. Said Smith:

> They are founded upon the most absurd of suppositions . . .
> the supposition that every successive generation of men have
> not an equal right to the earth, and to all that it possesses; but
> that the property of the present generation should be restrained
> and regulated according to the fancy of those who died perhaps
> five hundred years ago.

After communing with Cabanis and his progressive friends, Jefferson must have understood that conceptual analysis was the enlightened method of reasoning. Perhaps it was the realization that the pioneering Scottish economist felt exactly as he did about primogeniture and entailment that induced him to analyze these concepts.

Jefferson was sorting through and organizing a host of enlightened concepts when he went to Fontainebleau to attend the first of the king's fall levees in late-October of 1785. On the morning of the 27th, he set out "to take a view of the place. I shaped my course towards the highest of the mountains in sight, to the top of which was about a league." This brought Jefferson into the only interaction he recorded between himself and a member of France's poverty-stricken underclass. He "fell in with a poor woman walking at the same rate with myself and going the same course. Wishing to know the condition of the laboring poor I entered into conversation with her . . ."

In the course of his afternoon with the beggar woman, Jefferson discovered just how awful the poverty was that the poor people of France suffered. He knew they were poor, but until this encounter, he had managed keep them at a comfortable distance. He had labored quietly to eliminate land tenure in Virginia and had waged a private rebellion against encroachment by the King of England – and the squirearchy of Virginia – on his personal sovereignty. He had drafted a monumental work declaring the rights of man, ostensibly to protect individuals against this kind of depredation. But until he encountered the old hag near Fontainebleau he had no comprehension of the dimension of the evil he had been combating. Now he knew. To Madison, Jefferson wrote,

> *I am conscious that an equal division of property is*
> *impracticable, but the consequences of this enormous inequality*
> *producing so much misery to the bulk of mankind, legislators*
> *cannot invent too many devices for subdividing property, only*
> *taking care to let their subdivisions go hand in hand with the*
> *natural affections of the human mind.*

Four years later, Jefferson returned to the issue. This time he produced an entire argument against it. In it, he reasoned not from legal
precedent, but philosophically from premise to conclusion. More
remarkably, his premise was a concept. Briefly restated, his argument was this:

> *I set out on this ground, which I suppose to be self evident,*
> **"that the earth belongs in usufruct to the living;" that the**
> **dead have neither powers nor rights over it.** [Emphasis
> added] *The portion occupied by an individual ceases to be his*
> *when himself ceases to be, and reverts to the society.*

This premise, Jefferson asserted, implied this proposition:

> *no man can by **natural right** [Emphasis added] oblige the*
> *lands he occupied, or the persons who succeed him in that*
> *occupation, to the payment of debts contracted by him.*

This proposition established, he rejected the "habitual" practice in
which the public debts of one generation devolve on the next on the
grounds that

> ***this requisition is municipal only, not moral,*** [Emphasis added]
> *flowing from the will of the society which has found it convenient*
> *to appropriate the lands [when they] become vacant by the death*
> *of their occupant on the condition of a payment of his debts . . .*

Jefferson then asserted that the Law of Reason reveals

> *that between society and society, or generation and generation*

> *there is no municipal obligation, no umpire but the law of*
> *nature . . . by the law of nature, one generation is to another*
> *as one independent nation to another.*

Therefore,

> *no society can make a perpetual constitution, or even a perpetual*
> *law. The earth belongs always to the living generation . . . The*
> *constitution and the laws of their predecessors extinguished*
> *them, in their natural course [and] every constitution . . . and*
> *every law, naturally expires [with the generation that made it]*
> *at the end of 19 years.*

Jefferson concluded his letter by congratulating himself for "taking Reason for our guide instead of English precedents" (i.e., the Common Law) because doing this breaks the habit "which fetters us with all the political heresies of a nation."

The enlightened method of reasoning Jefferson used in this argument stands in stark contrast with the method he used prior to becoming enlightened. It was in a sense a breakthrough, but if Jefferson expected to impress his friend Madison with his new-model reasoning, he was sadly mistaken. The diminutive squire from Orange, Virginia, received Jefferson's groundbreaking analysis not long after succeeding in the almost impossible task of winning ratification for a new Constitution for the United States of America. He was justifiably proud of his work and of the form of government it embodied. The Father of the American Constitution was in no mood then, or ever after that, to indulge philosophers with lofty ideas about better forms of government.

Madison's response to Jefferson's was careful and cool. In the answer he wrote on February 4, 1790, he explained "the grounds of my skepticism" concerning Jefferson's idea for starting society and government over every 19 years. Madison summarized Jefferson's program this way:

> As the earth belongs to the living, not to the dead, a living generation can bind itself only: In every society the will of the majority binds the whole: According to the laws of mortality, a majority of those ripe at any moment for the exercise of their will do not live beyond nineteen years: To that term then is limited the validity of every act of the Society: Nor within that limitation, can any declaration of the public will be valid which is not express.

Madison responded to Jefferson's generality in three parts: 1) relating to "the fundamental Constitution of the Government; 2) "Laws involving stipulations which render them irrevocable at the will of the Legislature; and 3) "Laws involving no such irrevocable quality."

Concerning the first, Madison offered three crisp objections: 1) "a Government so often revised" would "become too mutable to retain those prejudices in its favor which antiquity inspires, and which are perhaps a salutary aid to the most rational Government," 2) such periodical revisions "would engender pernicious factions that might not otherwise come into existence," 3) a Government depending for its existence beyond a fixed date, on some positive and authentic intervention of the Society itself would be subject to "the casualty and consequences of an actual interregnum."

Regarding the second category, Madison offered these objections: 1) "improvements made by the dead form a charge against the living who take the benefit of them," 2) "debts may be incurred for purposes which interest the unborn, as well as the living", such as, for example, "debts for repelling a conquest," 3) debts may even be incurred principally for the benefit of posterity: such perhaps is the present debt of the United States, and "the term of 19 years might not be sufficient for discharging" them.

Madison summarized his objections to Jefferson's scheme in respect to the first two of his categories of law this way:

> There seems then to be a foundation in the nature of things, in the relation which one generation bears to another, for the descent of obligations from one to another. [But] equity requires it. Mutual good is promoted by it. All that is indispensable in adjusting the account between the dead & the living is to see that the debits against the latter do not exceed the advances made by the former. Few of the incumbrances entailed on Nations would bear a liquidation even on this principle.

In respect to Jefferson's third category of law, Madison noted that unless laws are kept in force by new acts, the rights depending on existing positive laws, including most rights of property, would become "defunct" and "the most violent struggles" would be "generated between those interested in reviving and those interested in new-modeling the former State of property." Additionally, "the obstacles to the passage of laws and the hazard of their rejection could lead to anarchy. This would undermine the value of property and contribute and "discourage the steady exertions of industry produced by permanent laws."

Madison concluded his analysis by politely dismissing Jefferson's impractical scheme. Said the Father of the American Constitution, "If the observations I have hazarded be not misapplied, it follows that a limitation of the validity of national acts to the computed life of a nation, is in some instances not required by Theory, and in others cannot be accommodated to practice."

This exchange illustrates the difference between an experienced political operative and a political solipsist turned reform-minded progressive. Perceiving the practical wisdom of Madison's analysis, and lacking reinforcement for his new mode of reasoning, Jefferson abandoned it. What remained from his enlightening experience in France was his dedication to the concept of progress and the moral imperative it entailed to lead his countrymen to enlightened perfection by whatever means were available.

chapter seventeen

Jefferson's Later Political Initiatives

*A*lthough he did not say so to Washington, Jefferson expected France's enlightened reformers to end the privilege of its hereditary aristocracy and replace its monarchical government with an American-styled republic.

Jefferson conceptualized this impending transition in terms of the revolution he had nominally begun in America. In Jefferson's enlightened view, the French people would assert their inalienable right to define their common good. They would exercise it by establishing a government in which they would elect the best and brightest among them to deliberate on their behalf and make the law. The laws they would make would reflect the will of the people. In this way, they would promote the freedom that Jefferson considered to be the necessary pre-condition for pursuing and achieving individual happiness.

Jefferson was in Paris when the people of France took their first steps in this glorious march of human progress. He left France, however, before his enlightened expectations could be shredded by the bloody reality of political warfare. He returned home a new political man with an inspired view of Reason as an instrument for solving the problems of man in society.

No sooner did he set foot on his native soil than he received the request of his President that he accept appointment as his country's first Secretary of State. This he did reluctantly on the insistence of his friend and trusted political advisor, James Madison. As a member of Washington's first cabinet, Jefferson discovered that he was in a circle of men who harbored "wrong" political ideas. The extent of the danger they posed became apparent to Jefferson as he familiarized himself with the fiscal policies of Washington's brilliant Secretary of the Treasury.

The conflict between Jefferson and Hamilton sharpened through a sequence of minor confrontations. The first was the matter of the arrears of pay still due those who bore arms during the War of American Independence. This was quickly overshadowed by the assumption issue.[1] Rightfully disturbed by Hamilton's announcement that the New England states considered assumption to be "a sine qua non of the continuance of the Union", Jefferson agreed to mediate in the dispute. A political solution was subsequently ironed out in a private dinner that Jefferson hosted for Hamilton and Madison. According to this "bargain", Jefferson (perhaps in the person of his trusted lieutenant) would deliver the votes necessary to pass a revised assumption bill in return for establishing the permanent seat of the federal government on the Potomac. This deal proved to be unpopular among southerners for a variety of reasons, not the least of which being that the government was to remain in Philadelphia for fifteen years.

---

[1]Northern states, which had paid off a smaller percentage of their war debts tended to favor their assumption by the federal government. Southern states, which had liquidated a larger percentage of these debts, tended to oppose the proposal.

The continued grumblings of Jefferson's political allies seems to have caused him to become uncomfortable with the deal he had orchestrated. For one thing, by making passage of Hamilton's measure possible, he had increased Hamilton's already considerable political power. Worse, he was beginning to see that Hamilton's fiscal policies would produce a hierarchical social structure based on capital. This would, of course, be detrimental to his agrarian society, which was by its nature based on debt. This diversion of interests exploded into an unresolvable political conflict in the winter of 1791 with the passage of a bill containing Hamilton's proposal that the federal government charter a bank.

Hamilton defended his plan on the grounds that the bank would build the credit worthiness of the government (which it now needed because of its obligations to liquidate the assumed war debts of the states). The opponents of the measure, led by Jefferson and Madison, contested it on the grounds that chartering such an institution was beyond the constitutional authority of the government.

There were other grounds for objection. The substantial bulk of the bank's funding was, for example, to be in the form of government-backed securities. It was to be under the management, however, of private individuals rather than public officials. Beyond that, there were no plans to establish branches in the credit-hungry south. Washington settled the dispute to the extent that on 25 February he signed the bill. Five days later, Jefferson offered a clerkship in his department to Philip Freneau, a staunch republican and noisy future critic of Hamiltonian policy.

Hamilton responded in kind as these attacks multiplied. A war of political words thus began. Jefferson no doubt took time to survey the political landscape as it intensified. At some point his gaze must have settled on the Electoral College whose vote decided the presidency. The math was easy enough to do. It showed that Jefferson's overwhelmingly southern adherents would command a majority in the Electoral College if their candidate could carry the state of New York. Was it co-incidence that on 17 May 1791, less than three months after Hamilton's pivotal victory on his bank measure, Jefferson set out from Philadelphia on what Malone describes as "a pleasure trip" to New England?

Jefferson stopped in New York City where Madison was waiting for him. The two men proceeded up the Hudson River Valley to Lake George. After a stormy sail on Lake Champlain, they toured Revolutionary War sites at Saratoga, Crown Point, Ticonderoga, and Bennington, Vermont. Turning south, they stopped at Pittsfield in western Massachusetts then descended the Connecticut River to Long Island Sound. Sailing around the island, they eventually reached Brooklyn and so returned to New York.

Malone dismisses the idea that this month-long tour had a political dimension. Following Jefferson's script, he asserts that Jefferson made it to restore his health and to make scientific observations. Hamilton's friends saw something more. "...There was every appearance of a passionate courtship between the Chancellor [Livingston], Burr, Jefferson & Madison when the two were in town," Robert Troup reported to Hamilton. [See: 15 June 1791; Hamilton Papers,

13:1724. Cited in Malone's *Jefferson and the Rights of Man.* Little Brown and Company. 1952. 382.]

Aaron Burr would upset the Federalist candidate, Revolutionary War hero General Philip Schuyler, and win a seat in the United States Senate a few months later. This was an unlikely outcome since the decision in Burr's favor was made in the Senate of New York, which was heavily Federalist in its political composition. Burr's success in these suspicious circumstances added to the distrust that both the Federalists and the anti-Federalists felt toward him.[2]

It is likely that Jefferson, with encouragement from Madison, wanted to know whether Burr was someone with whom members of the new Republican Party in Virginia could work. His conclusion was evidently mixed. Burr was a man of considerable talent and had conspicuous potential as a political leader. But there were other considerations. In addition to the question of his party loyalty, there was his staunch opposition to slavery and his support for women's suffrage. Whatever the reason, Jefferson did not warm to Burr as a political ally. Nor did he find the "ambitious" New Yorker personally

---

[2] Claude Bowers focused on this in Chapter VII of *Jefferson and Hamilton: The Struggle for Democracy.* He seems to contradict Malone by calling this chapter *Jefferson Mobilizes.* In it, he reconstructs the effort Jefferson made when he "assumed the task of organizing the opposition to the policies of the Federalists". "And Burr?" Bowers asks. "Just what Jefferson expected of Burr is a mystery unsolvable. He appreciated his brilliancy and professional prestige, *but were the penetrating eyes blind to the weakness of character?* Just a little while before Burr had joined with Hamilton against Clinton, and Federalist votes had sent him to the Senate." [*Jefferson and Hamilton: The Struggle for Democracy;* Houghton Mifflin Company. 1925.147. Emphasis added]

Character, In other words, was determined–at least in Burr's case–not by the good he may have produced for his community as a civic-minded private citizen and its duly elected representative, but by his loyalty to his party.

appealing, a discovery that may have cooled Jefferson's interest in becoming a candidate in the approaching Presidential election.

What of Burr's visit Monticello in early October of 1795? Burr's term in the Senate would end the following year. He was therefore looking ahead. Burr understood that Jefferson would be the Republican nominee for President in the election of 1796. His own credentials made him a legitimate candidate for Vice President on the Republican ticket. Indeed, the two men would constitute the Republican ticket in America's second Presidential election. Vice President John Adams would win it, and become the second President of the United States, with 71 electoral votes. Jefferson would receive 68 electoral votes and become the second Vice President. Burr would finish third with 30 electoral votes.

Burr undoubtedly traveled to Charlottesville in the fall of 1795 to apprise Jefferson of his interest to run, to assure Jefferson that he supported Jefferson for the first office, and to elicit Jefferson's support for his own candidacy. The fact that Burr departed the day after his arrival shows that their discussions were brief. Burr would have learned that Jefferson was not prepared to actively advance his own candidacy and that he was not inclined to help Burr. Having heard this, Burr departed.

Jefferson was an inactive candidate in the election of 1796. But during John Adams' presidency he established himself as the leader of the opposition party. By the election of 1800, he was prepared to be an active candidate. Thanks to Burr, their Republican ticket carried New York and so won the election. But there was a hitch—Burr and Jefferson received the same number of electoral votes. It was therefore up to the House of Representatives to decide which of the two men would be president. According to the rules the House adopted for settling this political crisis, each of the sixteen states would have one vote. Nine votes were therefore necessary to decide the presidency. On the first ballot, Jefferson received the votes of the eight states with Republican majorities. Burr received the votes of the six states with Federalist majorities. The states that divided on the candidates abstained. This is the way it remained through the next thirty-four ballots. "On the thirty sixth ballot the Federalists in the two divided states of Vermont and Maryland abstained, giving the vote of these states to Jefferson, who then had ten electoral votes. Delaware and South Carolina also abstained, being recorded as not voting. The other four New England states, by supporting Burr to the bitter end, suggested that they belonged to the Old Guard which preferred death to surrender." [See: Malone. *Jefferson and the Ordeal of Liberty.* 504.] This unyielding Federalist support for Burr came despite aggressive opposition from Alexander Hamilton.

Roger Kennedy gave this account of the conflict:

Jefferson was 'less dangerous because he 'will not dare much.' This was Hamilton's line against Jefferson. He was pusillanimous. But in order to head off Burr, Hamilton suggested that Jefferson's very weakness was in the national interest: Though he might not be 'very mindful of truth . . . and a contemptible hypocrite,' he was better than Burr, the 'most unfit and dangerous man in the community . . . profligate . . . voluptuary . . . [and] bankrupt.' Besides, as a 'hypocrite,' Jefferson might make a deal.

We ought–still to seek some advantages from our situation. It may be advisable to make it [strike-out] a ground of exploration with Mr. Jefferson or his confidential friends and the means of obtaining from him some assurances of his future conduct.

Hamilton then listed 'three essential points for us to secure,' and secure them the Federalists did from Mr. Jefferson's confidential friends. The Federalist could be satisfied that there would be no 'Revolution of 1800,' though Jefferson proclaimed to the world that there would be, and afterward that there had been. Bayard assured Samuel Smith that he would tip the balance for Jefferson if 'I had the assurance' on necessary points, and, on the following morning Smith returned, saying that 'he had seen Mr. Jefferson, . . . and was authorized by him to say that the Federal requirements corresponded with his views and intentions.' Bayard then brought over the pivotable electors to support Jefferson rather than Burr, on the thirty-sixth ballot. [See: Roger Kennedy. *Burr, Hamilton, and Jefferson – A Study in Character.* Oxford University Press, 2000. 78.]

Jefferson would spend his presidency–and years afterwards–settling the score with "the ambitious Mr. Burr." In the meantime, the success of Jefferson's political methods established a precedent for the modern political warfare that is celebrated today as "the democratic process." It was so bitter, and the political philosophies of the factions were so distant, that it divided the country. Jefferson's political sentiments were so strong that they killed his friendship with John Adams. The two men did not speak again until both had retired from politics and become disillusioned with the system they had created.

As president, Jefferson became so fearful that rising factionalism would destroy his new political society that he embraced a new social religion. "He was also responding to another problem that was of deep concern to him," Eugene Sheridan explains, "how to guarantee the perpetuation of republican government in the United States at a time when, as it seemed to him, political factionalism and social discord were threatening to undermine its basic foundation. Jefferson's solution to the problem was to foster the social harmony, which he considered essential for the survival of America's republican experiment. He did this by formulating a moralistic version of Christianity on which all men of good will could agree." [Dickinson W. Adams, Editor. Introduction by Eugene Sheridan. *Jefferson's Extracts from the Gospels.* Princeton University Press. 1983. 13.]

Jefferson was right to fear for his new political society. He was wrong, however, to think that adopting a new social religion would save it. Thirty-five years after his (and John Adams') death, the same factional differences that separated him from Hamilton caused the union to fail. The post-Jeffersonian system that was instituted after the suppression of the War for Southern Independence was no less vulnerable to the poisonous politics of faction. The destructiveness of this corrosive was, however, submerged during the westward expansion of the late-19th century and industrialization of the 20th century. The wealth generated in this unprecedented boom was enough to satisfy all the men who superintended the public good. By the beginning of the 20th century, America's post-Jeffersonian republic was safely in the hands of a neighborly political oligarchy that was too busy feasting on the riches of the new American empire to wage political warfare. Times have changed since then.

chapter eighteen

Old Jeffersonian Templates
and the New Thomas Jefferson

Collection • Description • Constructive Interpretation • Deconstruction
Separation • Legacy Management • Monument Psychoanalysis

Old Jeffersonian Templates

*T*homas Jefferson made himself interesting to history in 1776 by drafting the *Declaration of Independence.* He made himself a center of a controversy among his peers in Virginia soon after that by unveiling aplan to dismantle the socio-political hierarchy that allowed them to dominate all aspects of life in Virginia. His grandson, Thomas Jefferson Randolph launched the **Collection** phase of Jeffersonian historiography in 1829–30 by assembling and publishing the first edited collection of his grandfather's papers, *Memoir, Correspondence, and Miscellanies: from the Papers of Thomas Jefferson.* Randolph took on this task partly to defend his grandfather's reputation and partly to reduce the debt his bankrupt grandfather saddled on him. Jefferson's great granddaughter, Sarah Randolph, continued these efforts forty years later with *The Domestic Life of Thomas Jefferson* (1871).

A larger collection of Jefferson's papers, *The Writings of Thomas Jefferson: Being his Autobiography, Correspondence, Reports, Messages, Addresses, and Other Writings, Official and Private: Published by the Order of the Joint Committee of Congress on the Library, from the Original Manuscripts, Deposited in the Department of State,* was published by Taylor & Maury in Washington, D.C. in 1853. This collection contained "public" letters and documents that Library of Congress editors felt free to modify.

Paul Leicester Ford issued a 10-volume edition of Jefferson's letters between 1892 and 1896. In 1903–4, Andrew Adgate Lipscomb and Albert Ellery Bergh released a 20–volume collection. Lispcomb and Bergh built their expanded collection on the Library of Congress's bowdlerized edition. It therefore duplicated many of the parent's faults.

In 1858, Henry S. Randall launched the **Description** phase of Jeffersonian historiography when he published the first substantial biography of Thomas Jefferson. His three-volume work, *The Life of Thomas Jefferson,* was notable in part because it presented information gathered directly from members of Jefferson's family. This was followed in 1900 by Funk & Wagnall's *Jeffersonian Cyclopedia: A Comprehensive Collection of the Views of Thomas Jefferson,* edited by John P. Foley. This ambitious work itemized nine thousand facts about Thomas Jefferson.

Improvements in the collections of Jefferson's writings made it possible to discuss more aspects of Jefferson's life. The description phase of Jeffersonian historiography thus gained momentum through the first half the 20th century. Several admiring discussions of Jefferson appeared during this period. Notable among these were Fiske Kimball's *Thomas Jefferson Architect* (1916), Gilbert Chinard's *Thomas Jefferson: The Apostle of Americanism* (1929), and Claude Bowers' *Jefferson and Hamilton* (1925) and *Jefferson in Power* (1936). Bowers completed his set in 1945 with *The Young Jefferson.*

Carl Becker's *The Declaration of Independence* (1922) departed from these discussions in two notable ways. Becker focused on Jefferson's great work rather than on the man himself, and Becker insinuated a Jeffersonian philosophy. "The specific grievances enumerated in the Declaration," Becker reported, "were accordingly presented from the point of view of a carefully considered and resolutely held constitutional theory of the British empire. The essence of this theory, nowhere explicitly formulated in the Declaration, but throughout implicitly taken for granted, is that the colonies became parts of the empire by their own voluntary act, and remained parts of it solely by virtue of a compact subsisting between them and the king. Their rights were those of all men . . ." [Harcourt, Brace & Company. New York. 1922. 22.]

On the two hundredth anniversary of Jefferson's birth (1943), Princeton historian Julian Boyd began to write the last chapter in the Collection phase of Jeffersonian historiography. Boyd expanded the record to include all of Jefferson's incoming and outgoing correspondence, his personal notes, and drafts of his public documents. Boyd effectively merged Collection with Description by adding annotations and scholarly essays in which he discussed matters he considered particularly significant. The first volume of *The Papers of Thomas Jefferson* appeared in 1950. Boyd's successors expect to complete his project in 2030.

The Description phase of Jeffersonian historiography opened its last and longest chapter in 1948 when Dumas Malone began his detailed portrait of "the Father of Democracy in America." Malone's six-volume re-construction of Jefferson's life will probably never be surpassed for its comprehensive and complimentary treatment of the man. The work of a lifetime, Malone found virtue in all of his subject's undertakings and motives.

Boyd's collection provided a textual compliment to the shrine America's greatest progressive, President Franklin Delano Roosevelt, placed on the Tidal Basin adjacent to the Lincoln Memorial. Opening the same year Boyd commenced his massive project, the Jefferson Memorial presented the man as a monument to the American people. In his dedication address, President Roosevelt resurrected Thomas Jefferson politically, calling him "the Apostle of Freedom." "Leader in the philosophy of government, in education, in the arts, in efforts to lighten the toil of mankind—exponent of planning for the future," the iconic American President observed, "he led the steps of America into the path of the permanent integrity of the Republic." FDR did not tell the American public he was commissioning Thomas Jefferson to serve as the public face for his

New Deal. Perhaps it was because they were progressive themselves that Jeffersonian historiographers condoned this calculated deployment of their subject. As it happened, this carefully contrived political program conveyed a benefit to the stewards who maintained the public's memory of Thomas Jefferonson: it transformed them into de facto fellows of a national socio-political institute.

The fellows of this new institute responded by unveiling a new historiographical methodology. Jefferson's papers were being collected and annotated by Julian Boyd. Jefferson-the-man was being chronologized and roseated by Dumas Malone. Time had come to explicate *Jeffersonianism.* Early works in the field of **Constructive Interpretation** included Adrienne Koch's *The Philosophy of Thomas Jefferson* (1943), Karl Lehmann's *Thomas Jefferson – American Humanist* (1947), and Daniel Boorstein's *The Lost World of Thomas Jefferson* (1948), and Marie Kimball's *Jefferson – The Scene of Europe 1784–1789* (1950).

Professor Koch opened discussion on the topic that continues to dominate the conversations of Jeffersonian by analyzing the characteristics of Jefferson's thought. "History has been generous in singing Jefferson's praises," she explained in her introduction, "but we know how often praise obscures the man. The easy shibboleths 'democracy,' 'equality,' and 'the rights of man' have been used to enthrone him as a kind of vapid eighteenth-century saint (an unorthodox one, to be sure). Those who enjoy such a vision fail to see Jefferson in the true refinement and vigor of his thought. A more careful appraisal brings its reward to the student of ideas; for

Jefferson always had much to say . . ." [Quadrangle Paperback. Chicago. 1964. xiv.]

Professor Koch's thesis was neither history nor intellectual history. It was, as I say, constructive interpretation. One discovers reading Ms. Koch's pioneering text that Jefferson acquired most of what he knew about Philosophy, and everything else it seems, by himself in another room. The author was knowledgeable in respect to the sages she mentions, but she never manages to catch Jefferson in the act of exploring their ideas. At the outset of her discussion, she notes that Jefferson's so called *Commonplace Book of Philosophers and Poets* contains passages from "Homer, Euripides, Herodotus, and Anacreon; from Virgil, Ovid, Horace, Cicero, and Seneca." These were poets, historians, and statesmen. Where are the philosophers? Where are Jefferson's reflections on Plato's *Dialogues* and the virtues of his Socratic method? What did he think about Aristotle's *Metaphysics*? In Book Four, "The Philosopher" did after all present the principles of reasoning that form the foundations of Western civilization.

Did young Jefferson read works by Plato, or Aristotle, or their classical colleagues? Since their names are not in Professor Koch's text, it seems he did not. Why not? Jefferson was not an abstract thinker—he was not *philosophical.* Contrary to her intentions, Professor Koch shows that Jefferson was neither interested in Philosophy nor knew much about it. He deserves to be called as a philosopher, she argues, because he read a lot, thought a lot, and wrote a lot.

Harvard Professor B. F. Wright added this clarification to Professor Koch's discussion: "Jefferson 'was a man so vitally interested in exploring ideas that to deny him the title of 'philosopher' is to argue adherence to a prejudiced definition of the term.' Miss Koch thus states the central argument of her book. She does not claim for Jefferson any strikingly original contributions to the literature of philosophy or that his ideas add up to a system. Obviously, he wrote no technical treatise. She does contend that the variety and quality of the opinions expressed in his writings, particularly his letters, entitle him to serious consideration as one of the philosophical exponents of the Enlightenment." [Chicago Journals: Ethics. Vol. 54. No. 4 July 1944. 299.] These essential facts about Jefferson-the-philosopher are not repeated by the expositors of Jeffersonianism who followed Professor Koch.

The fact that Jefferson produced nothing "strictly original" and never synthesized his far-ranging opinions into a "technical treatise" did not deter constructive interpreters from developing Professor Koch's *philosopher* theme. The man who would succeed Malone as the Thomas Jefferson Foundation Professor of History at Mr. Jefferson's University certified it in 1960. Merrill Peterson's *The Jefferson Image in the American Mind* appeared as Malone was completing his monument. Peterson's text proved to be a first step in **Managing the Legacy** of the man Malone was apotheosizing. In it, Peterson identified the attribute that since then has defined the monument. Jefferson's legacy, Peterson proclaimed, "is the philosophy of human rights so eloquently stated in the Preamble of the Declaration of Independence." Peterson went on to affirm that "Jefferson is rapidly attaining the fame of world citizen some Americans were prophesying for him in 1943." Jeffersonianism thus became the framework for understanding America and the fellows of the institute became managers of America's Human Rights heritage business.

Professor Peterson's book appeared at the beginning of a generational change in American society. The war in Vietnam was about to begin and America's rising generation of comfortable, middle class college students did not want to fight it. As they resisted American "imperialism" (and the draft), blacks in the south and elsewhere began to resist racial discrimination. They were joined by women who demanded the right to control their own bodies and equal pay for equal work. Jeffersonians and progressives everywhere commended this uprising against white male control of American society. From their lofty perch on higher moral grounds, they encouraged the advance in the "philosophy of human rights" that Peterson had placed at the center of the Jeffersonian system.

Harvard Professor Bernard Bailyn certified these sentiments in *The Ideological Origins of the American Revolution* (1967). In this influential work, Professor Bailyn converted the American Revolution into the inaugural event in a grand Jeffersonian crusade. Oppressed American colonials, Bailyn discovered, acted on "an elevating transforming vision: a new, fresh, vigorous, and above all morally regenerate people rising from obscurity to defend the battlements of liberty and then in triumph standing forth, heartening and sustaining the cause of freedom everywhere."

This was Jefferson legacy management at its finest. Bailyn's interpretative view of Republicanism encompassed the ideas that progressives in colonial America launched an ongoing moral crusade to reform the world for the benefit of everyone in it; that the social unrest of the 1960s was a continuation of a morally-based Jeffersonian rebellion; and that his fellow "civic humanists" had a moral obligation to carry this great Jeffersonian work forward.

J.G.A. Pocock, Bailyn's partner in promoting a republican reinterpretation of American history, published *The Machiavellian Moment* (1975) eight years after Bailyn's masterwork appeared. Professor Pocock's frankensteinian creation resonated with academic progressives of the late 20th century. It is inconceivable, however, that 18th century colonials saw the world or their political movement through Pocock's lens. John Adams, while Ambassador to England, did refer to Machiavelli as "the great restorer of the true politics" (in his 3-volume *A Defence of the Constitutions of Government of the United States of America,* (1787)), but he also admired "Sidney, Locke, Harrington, Milton, Ponnet, the Vindiciae contra Tyrannos, Hoadley, Trenchard, Gordon, and Plato Redivivus." The rank and file of the patriotic movement, who probably never heard of Machiavelli, would have found Pocock's turgid discussion incomprehensible, as most of us do today.

What was Pocock's thesis? "The interpretation put forward here stresses Machiavelli at the expense of John Locke; it suggests that the republic—a concept derived from Renaissance humanism—was the true heir of the covenant and the dread of corruption the true heir of the jeremiad. It suggests that the foundation of independent America was seen, as stated, as taking place at a Machiavellian—even a Rousseauean—moment, at which the fragility of the experiment, and the ambiguity of the republic's position in secular time, was more vividly appreciated than it could been from a Lockean perspective." [Princeton University Press. 1975. 545.] None of this was topical for the insurgents who drank with Sam Adams at the Green Dragon Tavern in the years and months before Parliament closed the Port of Boston (on 1 June 1774). None of it was discussed by the troops who mustered after "the shot heard round the world" was fired (on 19 April 1776). But then Professor Pocock was not explicating their view either of themselves or the reasons they raised their rebellion.

Professors Bailyn and Pocock's republican-communitarian model provided a framework for the re-interpretation of the revolution their progressive associates were implementing. Their protégés would reconstruct America on their humanitarian principles. At the foundation of the new structure would be the figure in FDR's shrine—Thomas Jefferson-progressive-social-philosopher.

Professor Lance Banning's *The Jefferson Persuasion* (1978) was not strictly a biography of Jefferson. Professor Banning focused his attention on the political man who led the indictment of Federalism and the increasingly partisan campaigns of the 1790's in which Jefferson's new party battled to defend the republican principles upon which the new American government rested. "No one," Banning lamented, "has made a full-scale effort to comprehend the nature, sources, or importance of the [Republican] party's charge that the Republic was in danger."

Professor Richard Matthews seems to have answered this call. He began *The Radical Politics of Thomas Jefferson* (1984) saying, "This is a work of political theory. As such it is inherently interpretative as well as normative." Before explicating his theory, Professor Matthews did some needed housecleaning. In the first chapter of his refreshing text, he disposed of several renderings of "the philosophy of Thomas Jefferson" that had collected since Adrienne Koch opened the discussion in 1943. Having straightened up, Professor Matthews explained that "Jefferson's political philosophy possesses characteristics that are usually associated with three analytically separable traditions." [University Press of Kansas. 1986. 20.] These were, said Matthews, Humanism, Communitarian Anarchism, and Radical Democracy.

Professor Matthews' book was a marked improvement over interpretations like the one advanced by Professor Koch in the sense that he spoke about things that Jefferson did specifically discuss and endorse. Matthews, however, committed the same sin his predecessors committed by integrating them into a Jeffersonian "political theory". As Professor Wright correctly observed in 1944, Jefferson never organized his random thoughts into a treatise. He had a disposition and a repertoire of opinions, not a "system". Until he became enlightened, all of Jefferson's political initiatives were guided by a single rudimentary idea, one that came to him in the fall of 1774 while brooding alone over the Virginia Convention's rejection of the argument he advanced in his so called *Summary View of the Rights of British America*. Political power, young Jefferson decided then, must not be allowed to pool in the hands of tyrants. His political purpose, at least prior to his enlightenment, did not advance beyond this simple maxim.

By the time Professor Matthews' book appeared, the institute had become a gathering place for republicans. An advocate himself of the progressive republican ideology, Professor Matthew seemed less interested in locating the real Jefferson than in debunking the interpretation of America espoused by classical liberals. "The 'traditional' Jefferson," he announced in his concluding chapter, "continues to provide the legitimizing 'pretty,' if not beautiful drapery with which Americans quote the Declaration of Independence, but they live *The Federalist*. Myths die slowly . . . Jefferson is not in the possessive individualist tradition; and the traditional 'liberal' interpretations of him are in error." [Matthews. 120–121.]

Why is defining a Jeffersonian creed so important for republicans? A lot is at stake. Depending on who controls this high philosophical ground, Americans will learn either that they are individuals or parts of a community. Professor Bailyn understood this and designed American history to fit a properly Jeffersonian egalitarianism: the way to make the planet better is for Americans to quit envisioning themselves as exceptional individuals and to start seeing themselves as (ordinary) members of a global community.

The same year Matthews confirmed that Jefferson-the-political-theorist was a republican (1984), Charles Sanford unveiled Jefferson-the-moral-voyager. In *The Religious Life of Thomas Jefferson,* Sanford informed his readers that passing from worshiping in an organized church to a "youthful questioning about God" to private dissent to rejecting God's agency in the affairs of men were all aspects of Jefferson's "religious" development. "His commonplace notebook shows," Sanford continued, "that he was reading widely in literature, political philosophy, the classics, law, and history to learn the nature of man and the origins of human government and society. He was laying the groundwork for his religious, political, and social convictions that were to be the basis of his inner life and career and preparing himself for his role as one of the political and philosophical leaders of the American Revolution." In other words, Professor Sanford encountered the autodidact Professor Koch pictured learning philosophy in the next room. To this persona, Sanford added a bold new dimension. Another essential aspect of Jefferson's self-enlightenment was his abandonment of faith in God and the apotheosis of Reason.

In 1986, Henry Steele Commager, then considered "our most broad-ranging American historian," published *Jefferson, Nationalism and the Enlightenment.* Commager elevated the morally alert political theorist into the symbolic center of the Enlightenment and an 18th century model of Plato's philosopher king. Commager hailed an intellectual who was also a public man who could write the *Declaration of Independence,* serve as President of the United States, and create the University of Virginia while studying agriculture, law, religion, literature, and the foundations of right behavior.

Noble Cunningham reinforced the idea that Jefferson was the man for all seasons in *In Pursuit of Reason: The Life of Thomas Jefferson* (1987). "Certain basic tenets," Cunningham announced, "motivated his life and shaped his actions in whatever challenge he faced. Of these, none was stronger than his belief in the sufficiency of reason for the care of human affairs." Cunningham's self-appointed mission was to make scholars and students alike appreciate the rational Jefferson.

Four years later, Garrett Sheldon published *The Political Philosophy of Thomas Jefferson* (1991). Professor Sheldon offered an analysis of "the historical development of Thomas Jefferson's political philosophy within the context of the major themes of Western political theory and the contemporary historiographic debates over early American political thought." Sheldon was, in other words, attempting to bridge the chasm that now separated the institute's dominant republican ideology (with its emphasis on the common good) from the classical liberalism (with its emphasis on individual rights) implicit in the massive work of Dumas Malone.

Professor Herbert Sloan appreciated the danger this division posed for the well being of his institute. In *Principle & Interest: Thomas Jefferson & the Problem of Debt* (1995), he began his discussion on Jefferson and debt by observing that, "we are beginning to entertain the possibility that the republican and country party Jefferson of Banning and Murrin does not automatically exclude the liberal Jefferson of Appleby." Professor Sloan did not mention that the division between Republicans and Liberals had degenerated into a cold war mostly because the progressive ideologues who dominated the institute wanted to purge it of its liberal holders on. The problem went beyond sociability. Progressives preferred for the community of man to be managed by their ideological allies. Classical liberals were more or less content for the leviathan to lumber along on its own haphazard course. The future of mankind and the fate of the planet hung in the balance!

In keeping with this progressive imperative, Jeffersonian legacy managers raised their game to the next level. By 1995, their discussions centered on the constructive impact Jeffersonian principles could have on the world at large. Expositors of this higher level Jeffersonianism produced analyses that drew on concepts framed by their colleagues. New analyses referred to friendly old analyses, which became doctrinal through scholarly citation. Constructive interpretation thus elevated the institute and its monument while the man beneath them quietly faded from view.

Malone was putting the finishing touches on his monument and the fellows of the institute were coming into stride managing Jefferson's republican legacy when Fawn Brodie published a book called *Thomas Jefferson – An Intimate History* (1974). This king's-new-clothes biography marked the beginning of the age of **Deconstruction** that quickly undermined the edifice Malone had spent his professional career building. It also threatened the institute that managed *The Legacy* and embarrassed progressives who were discerning the marvelous ways Jeffersonian republicanism could improve the world.

Professor Brodie impugned all of them by raising questions about the man's relationship with one of his slaves. Jefferson owned Sally Hemings. Sally Hemings was (supposedly) the half sister of Jefferson's deceased wife. Thomas Jefferson owned his wife's half-sister. But that was not all. He sired a number of children on her. And he kept them enslaved. If the scholars at Thomas Jefferson's Monticello are correct, Jefferson kept his own children enslaved!

Brodie's unwelcomed commentary reminded the public that Jefferson was not a monument after all. Nor was he just a man. Professor Brodie showed America and the world that Thomas Jefferson was a man with a history that did not jibe with his lately blossomed progressive political philosophy. Old school Jeffersonians quickly condemned Professor Brodie's work as "psycho-history". *The Washington Post* made it plain, however, that the issue was not going away by defending Brodie's work as "brilliant and provocative".

The deconstruction that Brodie started continued through the last quarter of the 20th century. In *The Wolfe by the Ears* (1991), John Chester Miller conducted a sympathetic investigation of Jefferson's life as a slaveholder. Conor Cruise O'Brien was not so kind. In *The Long Affair* (1996), O'Brien angrily condemned

Jefferson for being an apologist for the "genocide" of the French Revolution and a latent white supremacist. Annette Gordon-Reed redirected and broadened the conversation about Jefferson's "racism" in *Thomas Jefferson and Sally Hemings: An American Controversy,* (1997). "The more important feature of the Jefferson-Hemings debate," Professor Gordon-Reed opined, "was what it said about the views of Americans, and it must be said, some white Americans, about the proper relationships between blacks and whites." Jefferson, of course, helped to shape America's views regarding "the proper relationships between blacks and whites" with opinions he expressed in Query XIV of his venerated *Notes on the State of Virginia* (first published in 1785).

Professors Peter Onuf and Jan Lewis presumed to settle these matters with the essay collection they produced two years later (*Sally Hemings and Thomas Jefferson: History, Memory, and Civic Culture,* 1999). "At most," they concluded in their Introduction, "the scientific evidence, which in itself is far from definitive, only confirmed what traditional sources as well as our professional judgment had suggested: some sort of long-term relationship existed between Jefferson and the slave woman . . . rumored to have been his concubine."

In her introduction to *American Scripture,* which appeared the same year as Professor Gordon-Reed's book, Professor Pauline Maier echoed the new scholarly protocol—coolness towards dead white men. "It does strike me as odd," she said, "that historians' obsession with Jefferson continues unabated at a time when studying the history of 'great white men' has become unfashionable in the profession. As this book makes plain, I dissent from any suggestion that Jefferson was alone responsible for the Declaration of Independence, or that the document most worth studying and admiring is his draft, or that the full story of the declaration can be told apart from that of the Independence it declared and the process that led to it."

After Professor Brodie's psychohistory, one finds few if any works that compliment Jefferson without qualification. Forrest McDonald might be considered the leader of the last-stand traditionalists. Prof. McDonald noticed that "precious little" in the huge volume of Jefferson scholarship dealt with Jefferson's presidency. He addressed this problem in 1974 in *The Presidency of Thomas Jefferson*. "Unlike most historians," McDonald reported in his preface, I "am more interested in what he did than in what . . . he said or thought." Other works that fall into this genre are Merrill Peterson's *Adams and Jefferson – A Revolutionary Dialogue* (1976), Frank Dewey's *Thomas Jefferson, Lawyer* (1986), Jack McLaughlin's *Jefferson and Monticello* (1988), George Green Shackelford's *Thomas Jefferson's Travels in Europe, 1784–1789* (1993) and William Howard Adams' *The Paris Years of Thomas Jefferson,* (1997).

David Mayer provided a helpful bridge that connects Banning's political man to Cunningham's rationalist in his informative *The Constitutional Thought of Thomas Jefferson* (1994). Joseph Ellis continued in this vein by illuminating "Jefferson's character, the animating principles that informed his public and private life and made him the significant statesman and distinctive man that he was" in *The American Sphinx* (1998). Ellis undertook to do this by revealing "a core of convictions and apprehensions" as they expressed themselves at "propitious moments of his life". What Joseph Ellis described as "Jefferson's paradoxical stance on slavery" remained, nevertheless, as a reason for the fellows of the institute to keep him off Malone's pedestal.

In the fall of 1992, Peter Onuf, then Thomas Jefferson Foundation Professor of History at the University of Virginia, convened a conference to commemorate the 250th anniversary of Jefferson's birth. "The premise of the conference," Professor Onuf reported in the foreword of the anthology of papers presented at the conclave (*Jeffersonian Legacies,* 1993), "was that Jefferson's legacies—for better or worse—are directly relevant to some of the most crucial concerns of America in the 1990s. If women's rights and racial tension are burning issues today, what can be learned about them from Thomas Jefferson?" This groundbreaking collection might be counted as the first work in a new Jeffersonian historiography. I call it **Separation.**

Fourteen years later, after the fellows of the institute had distanced themselves from the man they had spent decades apotheosizing, Professor Onuf brought out *The Mind of Thomas* (2007). "I hope to spark some conversations with and about Thomas Jefferson," Professor Onuf explained in its introduction, "to engage the rich and complex legacy he has left us in his voluminous correspondence as well as in the great public papers that have played and will play such a crucial role in defining the meaning and purposes of American nationhood." This comment alludes to the institute's post-Brodie approach: maximize The Legacy, minimize The Man. "There are encouraging signs," Professor Onuf hoped, "that Jefferson scholarship is finally breaking free from this vicious circle of celebration and condemnation. As the historiographical essays in this book suggest, we know more now—and can speculate more intelligently—about the private Jefferson than ever before." This is hardly encouraging news from an institute that spent a generation deliberately ignoring Jefferson's slave problem.

The Cambridge Companion to Thomas Jefferson, edited by Professor Frank Shuffelton, appeared two years after Professor Onuf's book. "The Scholarship supporting this work," Professor Shuffelton announced, "has been grounded in new strategies of interpretation in some cases, and new recognitions of larger intellectual and ideological contexts in which Jefferson wrote. Scholarship in the last thirty years has by turns addressed the significance of the republican synthesis, the role of classical liberalism, the importance of moral sentiment and sentimentality, the prevailing code of honor among gentlemen, and the discourse of sociability and the public sphere. Jefferson's texts have been deconstructed, psychoanalyzed, and examined for participation in various hegemonic strategies, they have been read closely in order to unpack the metaphors and tropes that might give insight into the mind of Jefferson and the mind of his time . . . in the supposed death bed words of John Adams, 'Thomas Jefferson still survives,' if not as the icon he once was then as a touchstone able to generate continuing interest, debates, and inquiry. *This volume addresses major topics of Jeffersonian concern that may well reflect the concerns of Americans in the twenty-first century."* [Emphasis added] In other words, Jeffersonian fellows, having got clear of Jefferson-the-man and moved beyond the slave thing, were ready to resume their institutional mission of managing The Legacy.

Professor Francis Cogliano seemed to confirm this in his introduction to *A Companion to Thomas Jefferson* (2011). "In October 1992 Peter S. Onuf, the Thomas Jefferson Foundation Professor at the University of Virginia, organized a six-day conference to commemorate the anniversary of Jefferson's birth. Arising from that conference was an essay collection, *Jeffersonian Legacies,* which presented fifteen essays by leading scholars focusing on different aspects of Jefferson's life and legacy . . . Nearly a generation has passed since its publication . . . *The present volume can be read as a sequel to* **Jeffersonian Legacies,** *which aims to take stock of the vast and growing scholarly literature on Jefferson and to offer fresh insights from leading scholars on Jefferson and his time."* [Emphasis added]

The mission may be unchanged, but its "scholarly literature" suggests that a new era in Jefferson legacy management is dawning. Early indications are that we have entered the age of **Monument**

Psychoanalysis. Three works in this genre have been published since 2011: *The Limits of Optimism – Thomas Jefferson's Dualistic Enlightenment* (2011) by Professor Maurizio Valsania, *Thomas Jefferson, Time, and History* (2011) by Professor Hannah Spahn, and *Nature's Man: Thomas Jefferson's Philosophical Anthropology* (2013) also by Professor Valsania. All of these new-age commentaries are in the University Press of Virginia's *Jeffersonian America* series. The hierarchs of Jeffersonianism are, in other words, the sponsors of the new historiography. At first glance, this seems odd. Why? Because it deconstructs the monument Jeffersonian Legacy managers have spent the last two decades creating.

"Beneath the masculine overconfidence that Jefferson so often wielded," Professor Valsania explains in the first book, "it is quite interesting to detect 'differences.' Tremors of reservation, a sense of the tragic and even blatant pessimism lies beneath Jefferson's famous rhetoric of optimism. A fundamental tension thwarted Jefferson's peace of mind, and it was by no means occasional. The tension to which I am alluding is typical of the Enlightenment as a whole."

Readers of Professor Valsania's analysis will have a difficult time understanding what he is talking about. One reason is that he does not ground his analysis in fact. He does not explain, for example, what it was for men in the 18th century to be "enlightened". Instead he talks about "the hope of progress" and laments that, in Jefferson's case, this "optimism" faded on bad days. Readers of this book will not know that as Thomas Jefferson advanced through life he acquired new knowledge and new insights into the nature of things.

They will not know that his consequential ideas, unsystematized as they purportedly were, were underpinned by core beliefs and convictions.

Professor Spahn's psychohistory is filled with the jargon Professor Valsania used. "Even the most 'progressive' eighteenth-century minds . . . took for granted, far more than the Romantic image of the Enlightenment's philosophical hubris seems to suggest in retrospect, fundamental limitations in the pursuit of secular progress." For the record, the 18th century Enlightenment was not led by men who thought there were "fundamental limitations in the pursuit of secular progress." Philosophers would call Professor Spahn's claim a "straw man", meaning a false representation or a misrepresentation of the subject in question. Her book has a more conspicuous weakness: it says nothing substantive about Thomas Jefferson. "Jefferson," the author explains, "was a consummate product of [a] Newtonian culture. The self-consciously approximative character of his empiricism extended to the details of his approach to time . . . Jefferson's writings derive their philosophical relevance and their contradictory beauty from the fact that while he sought to emulate his cultural ideal of a versatile, open-minded Enlightenment, he was becoming sensitive to the intellectual tensions it created."

The stewards of the Jeffersonian legacy have approved publication of Ms. Spahn's book, it seems, on the chance that her analysis will divert attention from the problem that has tainted their business since Fawn Brodie broke the news that Jefferson fathered children on his deceased wife's enslaved half-sister. Since Fawn Brodie's controversial book appeared, Jeffersonian legacy managers have had the impossible task of condemning the man who kept his beloved and their bi-racial children enslaved while, at the same time, celebrating the visionary who invented Human Rights. Professor Spahn attempts to circumvent this unbridgeable contradiction by detecting a new problem: poor Tom had to "come to terms with the decisive problem of historical change." Fellows of the institute may find her analysis useful for developing new lines of scholarly conversation. Few members of the inquiring public will it profit from it, however. Where is the value in knowing that Jefferson-the-monument had a psychological problem?

In *Nature's Man: Thomas Jefferson's Philosophical Anthropology*, Professor Valsania cultivates the seed he planted in *The Limits of Optimism*. Discerning readers will notice that he is building on Professor Spahn's straw man. He is, briefly put, reconfiguring the Enlightenment to fit with contemporary cosmopolitanism. His dust cover tells us why. Professor Valsania's exploration "touches on Jefferson's concepts of nationalism, slavery, gender roles, modernity, affiliation, and community. More than that, *Nature's Man* shows how Jefferson could advocate equality and yet control and own other human beings."

"The eighteenth-century Enlightenment, both in Europe and in the United States," Professor Valsania reports, "represented a reaction against every form of precritical rationalism." He moves from this sketchy base into invention. The Enlightenment, he continues, was also a reaction "against the allegation that human faculties could solve—or, at least, justify—all flaws of existence." The Enlightenment was many things, but nowhere was it a rejection of the idea that men could solve the problems of society. In France for example, it was powered by an idea exactly antithetical to this. Professor Valzania should have read Turgot and the works of Turgot's progressive protégé, Marie Jean Caritat, marquis de Condorcet.

In *A Philosophical Review of the Successive Advances of the Human Mind* (1750), Turgot unveiled the idea that became the cornerstone of the French Enlightenment. It was what Jefferson learned while communing with the duc de la Rochefoucauld and Condorcet and their circle of chateau reformers. "Finally," Turgot observed, "commercial and political ties unite all parts of the globe, and the whole human race, through alternate periods of rest and unrest, of weal and woe, goes on advancing, although at a slow pace, towards greater perfection." [R. L. Meek. *Turgot.* Cambridge. 1973. 41.] Condorcet fixed this idea in the center of Turgot's *philosophy:* " . . . he proves, from the unbounded perfectibility which he attributes to the human understanding, that no limits can be prescribed to the improvement of the sciences. This opinion, which he never once abandoned, was one of the great principles of his philosophy." [*Life of Turgot.* London, 1787.]

Condorcet is remembered today for crystalizing his mentor's enlightened concept into the so-called Doctrine of Progress. In the introduction to his masterpiece, which he wore in the desperate weeks before taking his own life, Condorcet said this:

> *There remains . . . a third picture to form—that of our hopes, or*
> *the progress reserved for future generations, which the constancy*
> *of the laws of nature seems to secure to mankind . . . it will be*
> *necessary to shew by what steps this progress . . . is gradually to be*
> *rendered possible, and even easy; . . . by what ties nature has*
> *undissolubly united the advancement of knowledge with the*
> *progress of liberty, virtue, and respect for the rights of man . . .*
> [Introduction, *Outlines of an Historical View of the Progress of*
> *the Human Mind.* Translation for Carey, Rice & co. 1796. 13.
> From Liberty Library.]

In the final section of his essay, the Tenth Epoch, Condorcet added this:

> *All the causes which contribute to the improvement of the human*
> *species, all the means we have enumerated that insure its progress,*
> *must, from their very nature, exercise an influence always active,*
> *and acquire an extent for ever increasing. The proofs of this have*
> *been exhibited, and from their development in the work itself*
> *they will derive additional force:* ***accordingly we may already***
> ***conclude, that the perfectibility of man is indefinite . . .*** [Ibid.
> 135.] [Emphasis added]

This was the worldview of the men in Thomas Jefferson's French circles. It was the worldview Jefferson digested and embraced as he groomed himself to join their exclusive society. It was the worldview that underpinned his campaign for President in 1800, and it guided him after his election. Professor Valsania does not understand this. Nor does he provide other useful insights about Jefferson's connection to the "Enlightenment". His psychoanalysis may be useful to Jeffersonian legacy managers, but readers from the inquiring public will learn only that the newest Jeffersonian historiography has no tangible connection to reality.

The New Thomas Jefferson

I am a philosopher, not an historian. I find Thomas Jefferson interesting not because of his legacy but because he interacted with creative thinkers. Acouple of his compatriots in the independence movement, for example, formulated the Natural Rights argument he incorporated into the preamble of the American *Declaration of Independence.* During his sojourn to France, he joined a circle of philosophes who were crystalizing the idea that the history of man in society is a slow-gathering advance toward theoretical perfection. After he returned from France, he associated with men who organized America's first political party and launched a campaign that changed America from a *civil* society into a *political* society.

I separate myself from the ideologues and psychoanalysts discussed in the previous section by answering a comparatively mundane question: How did Thomas Jefferson become enlightened? I leave it to Jefferson to answer this question, which he does in conversations with his French enlighteners. This strikes me as the best way to show readers how Jefferson changed during his sojourn in France. I call it **non-fiction narration.** It is a substantive alternative to the humanistic creationism that Jeffersonian legacy management has become.

Readers of *Thomas Jefferson's Enlightenment – Paris 1785* accompany the novice diplomat as he integrates himself into the world's most cultured and extravagant society. They listen as celebrated French *lumieres* introduce him to their concept of Progress. They see what he sees as he travels through the bustling, reeking thoroughfares of Paris. The aspiring American did not do these things alone in his rooms. He had the assistance of enlightened companions.

I begin my narrative by setting the intellectual stage. I explain that the Enlightenment was a series of distinctive events. I recognize the importance of Freemasonry as an enlightening impulse and identify the Freemasons who enlightened Jefferson. I explain that after declaring American independence, Jefferson spent most of his time during the American Revolution rebelling against the pseudo-aristocrats who dominated society in colonial Virginia. I explain why Jefferson's "other rebellion" was the center of his attention and why it caused him to become what I call a political solipsist. I explain how Jefferson's rebellions roiled the waters of his domestic affairs and why his wife's premature death affected him the way it did. I explain the connection between his wife's death and his decision to go to France, what he intended to accomplish there, and how he planned to accomplish it.

Jefferson's relationships with the men and women in his French circles may not seem like things a philosopher would care about, but these were the people who instilled in Jefferson the vision that inspired a political solipsist to become a candidate in his country's first national political campaign. If we want to understand how this happened, we need to know who Jefferson's enlighteners were, what they thought, and the influence they exerted on the mountain man from the American frontier. In my opinion, this is the way to learn history: know the people who produced it and how they influenced each other.

Like every real person, the Jefferson we follow through Paris knows a lot about some things and little or nothing about many others. He was therefore fortunate to be befriended by one of the best-informed men in pre-revolutionary France. Because Pierre Cabanis was intimately familiar with the elements of the French concept of *Progress,* he was able to reconstruct it for Jefferson. Equally valuable to the American adventurer were Cabanis' friendships with the prominent figures in the salon society Jefferson went to France to join. With Cabanis' assistance, Jefferson accomplished what he set out to do. He became a Renaissance man and a member of Chastellux's exclusive social set.

We do not hear much about "the rights of man" from Jefferson while he is being enlightened. The man who arrived in France in the fall of the preceding year had been trained in the English Common Law and distinguished himself by compiling and enumerating, not by philosophizing. Oddly enough, the mountain man who arrived in France in August of 1784 had no pressing interest in or penetrating insight into the Rights of Man. Public right was for pre-enlightened Thomas Jefferson a Common Law issue that had been settled during the six centuries England muddled through after Magna Carta.

By the fall of 1785, Jefferson had digested the French concept of Progress. When a few of the best men in Paris were satisfied that he shared their progressive view of the world, they invited him to join their quiet effort to reform French society. It was after he became a member of this exclusive circle that Jefferson's interest in the rights of man crystalized. This concept, the distinguishing asset of Jefferson-the-monument, came into focus for Jefferson-the-man **after** the Assembly of Notables met in the winter of 1787. A member then of an elite circle of progressives, Jefferson embraced their implausible expectation that all the problems of French society would resolve themselves once France's oppressive monarchy had been replaced by a constitutional government with a properly formed Bill of Rights.

Since Jefferson's aristocratic cohorts knew comparatively little about public right and even less about constitutional government, they consulted the author of the *Declaration of Independence.* Flattered by their deference to his views on these weighty matters, Jefferson drew back in veil and stepped forward. When he returned to America in September of 1789, he brought with him the concept of himself as an illuminated reformer whose mission was to lead the people down the enlightened path to of progress.

In Paris in late 1785, Jefferson entered an intellectual circle unlike anything he had known in America. It was filled with disengaged men who reflected and theorized. It was led by the brilliant and opinionated marquis de Condorcet. Inspired by his far-ranging speculations, Jefferson began to dabble himself in philosophical abstraction. "The earth belongs to the living" is his only memorable philosophical revelation. James Madison, at least, was not impressed.

The capacity to abstract and philosophize did not become a Jeffersonian strength until after the man had been transfigured into a monument in the mid-20th century. A lot of hot air was used to inflate this monumental balloon. The real Thomas Jefferson was just a man who, like the rest of us, had strengths and weaknesses. He was aspiring, finite, and understandable. Readers of *Thomas Jefferson's Enlightenment* will find the world Jefferson entered in the summer of 1784 a fascinating spectacle. They will learn that during the five years he spent in it, Jefferson associated with men and women who were rich, idealistic, and sometimes as brilliant as he. Because Jefferson wanted to be admired by them, he adopted their view of the world. In this process, he accidently prepared himself to become the third President of the United States – and a national monument.